A Culture
of Peace

A CULTURE OF PEACE

God's Vision for the Church

*Alan Kreider, Eleanor Kreider,
and Paulus Widjaja*

Published in cooperation with
Mennonite World Conference

Good Books®

Intercourse, PA 17534
800/762-7171
www.GoodBks.com

A Culture of Peace: God's Vision for the Church is published in cooperation with Mennonite World Conference (MWC) and has been selected for its Global Anabaptist-Mennonite Shelf of Literature. MWC chooses one book each year and urges its member churches to translate and study the book, in an effort to develop a common body of literature.

Mennonite World Conference is a global community of Christian churches who trace their beginning to the 16th-century Radical Reformation in Europe, particularly to the Anabaptist movement. Today, close to 1,300,000 believers belong to this faith family; at least 60 percent are African, Asian, or Latin American.

MWC represents 95 Mennonite and Brethren in Christ national churches from 51 countries on six continents.

Mennonite World Conference exists to (1) be a global community of faith in the Anabaptist tradition, (2) facilitate community among Anabaptist-related churches worldwide, and (3) relate to other Christian world communions and organizations.

MWC's headquarters are in Strasbourg, France. For more information, visit its website at www.mwc-cmm.org.

Acknowledgments

We would like to thank many friends who, with their comments and insights, have strengthened this book: notably Stuart Murray Williams, of the Anabaptist Network in the U.K., who has read the entire manuscript and done much to clarify our ideas; Alastair McKay, of the Bridge Builders program of the London Mennonite Centre, whose insights into conflict transformation have strengthened Chapter 5; and Willard M. Swartley of the Associated Mennonite Biblical Seminary, who has provided valuable counsel on our use of the Bible. All errors and indiscretions which remain are those of the authors.

All biblical citations are from the *New Revised Standard Version Bible*, copyright © 1989 by the Division of Christian Education of the National Council of the Churches of Christ in the United States of America. Used by permission. All rights reserved.

Permission to include Appendix I, "Agreeing and Disagreeing in Love," has been granted by the Mennonite Church USA.

Cover photo: © Paul Hardy/CORBIS.

Library of Congress Cataloging-in-Publication Data
Kreider, Alan
   A culture of peace : God's vision for the church / Alan Kreider, Eleanor
Kreider, and Paulus Widjaja.
      p. cm.
   ISBN 1-56148-504-7 (pbk.)
   1. Peace--Religious aspects—Christianity. 2. Christian life. 3. Reconciliation—Religious
aspects—Christianity. 4. Church. I. Kreider, Eleanor, II. Widjaja, Paulus. III. Title.
   BT736.4.K75 2005
   261.8'73--dc22   2005024596

Table of Contents

Introduction

This book was conceived in an airport. On a rainy Indonesian evening in July 1993, Paulus Widjaja met our plane at the Semarang airport. During the next few days, as Eleanor and I worked closely with Paulus and had long conversations, we sensed a special affinity. One of Paulus's comments made a deep impression on us: "If the Christian church is to make any impact on Indonesia, it must address itself to the church's biggest peace issue—reconciliation with the Muslims."

This book also has origins in England. As Eleanor and I were entering the final stage of our 30 years of work as missionary teachers in England, I was on retreat in an Anglican Benedictine monastery. I was reading the first verses of Philippians 1: "Paul and Timothy, servants of Christ Jesus, to all the saints in Christ Jesus who are in Philippi, with the bishops and deacons: Grace to you and peace from God our Father and the Lord Jesus Christ."

I don't know how often I have read that verse, but it suddenly was clear to me. Paul, in writing to a church that he valued, blesses them twice: with "grace and peace." Grace and peace—a potent combination. How many epistles, I wondered, begin like that? So I began to check and discovered that almost all of them do. Then I paused. If Paul and Peter both began their letters like this, both grace and peace must be important.

So Eleanor and I set out to clarify our understandings of grace and peace in the Bible and to see how these could be applied to the life of the typical congregation. As we interacted with churches of many denominations, we came to be increasingly convinced that the "gospel of peace" (Acts 10:36) is true—and it is good news. It applies to every area of the church's life: to the relationship between its members and God, to the relationships of its members with each other, to its life of worship, to the way its members do their work, respond to war, and share their faith.

We presented our ideas to many groups, and their responses developed our ideas and gave us many illustrations. Early versions of our teaching appeared in *Anabaptism Today*, the journal of the U.K. Anabaptist Network;[1] and eventually these appeared in a booklet, *Becoming a Peace Church*.[2] When we moved back to our native U.S., we once again gave our teachings in many churches not only in the U.S., but also in Canada, Japan, Korea, Taiwan, and Hong Kong.

Meanwhile, Paulus finished his doctoral studies at Fuller Theological Seminary and returned to Indonesia, where he received a challenge and an honor: he was appointed Director of the Center for the Study and Promotion of Peace at Duta Wacana Christian University in Jogjakarta. Quickly Paulus discovered that his earlier intuitions were right: Christians were indeed able to make many contributions to peace in Indonesia. He taught peacemaking to people who were preparing for the Christian ministry; he also trained people in the skills of conflict transformation, and he was himself involved in tense situations that required faith and hope as well as skill.

Paulus had also become Secretary of the Peace Council of Mennonite World Conference. In 2003, at the invitation of Mennonite World Conference, I went to Jogjakarta to work with Paulus and the Associate Secretary of the Peace Council, Judy Zimmerman Herr. We prepared a paper for the Assembly of Anabaptist/Mennonite Christians from many countries, meeting that year in Bulawayo, Zimbabwe. Together, Paulus, Judy, and I studied the statements that Anabaptist/Mennonite national conferences from many parts of the world made about the role of peace in their lives. All three of us were inspired by these stories, which indicated to us that the global Anabaptist/Mennonite family is becoming a peace church. And it was gratifying to see Paulus, with his colleagues in Jogjakarta, finding life in the joys and struggles of grace- and peace-making.

In 2004 Paulus, Eleanor and I met again, in Pennsylvania, this time to work together on this book. First we brainstormed. For several days Paulus, Eleanor, and I exchanged ideas, and Eleanor and I took detailed notes. Then I revised our booklet, *Becoming a Peace Church*, in light of our discussions, and Eleanor revised the revision, which we spirited electronically to Paulus in Indonesia. Paulus was working under considerable strain; he had new courses to teach and conflicts to mediate. In January of 2005 the Center where he is Director was overwhelmed by the needs for trauma counseling in the aftermath of the catastrophic earthquake and tsunami in Aceh province. Nevertheless, despite these demands, Paulus produced remarkable work. He revised what we had written, and he added many pages of new material that give his theological insights and tell stories of his hands-on experience in Indonesia.

Why did we choose to write about "cultures of peace" instead of "peace churches"? For three reasons. First, because thinkers in various Christian traditions have recently begun to use the term *culture* to describe the life of the church. Influential Christians, beginning with the late Pope John Paul II, have called the church to be a "culture of life"; other writers have begun to use the term "cultures of peace."[3]

Second, because culture is an immensely rich term. Anthropologists speak of culture as "webs of meaning" that we humans live within, that we ourselves have "spun." The webs of language, beliefs, institutions, and practices enable us to function in ways that are necessary for us to flourish and be at home.[4] So we ask of the dynamic, changing cultures that we live in: are our cultures hospitable? Can we and others be whole and at home in them? In this book we are presenting a vision of the church as a culture of peace. We believe that this is a culture that God is creating—a hospitable culture.

Third, because culture grows out of our stories. English Baptist theologian Paul S. Fiddes is convinced that cultures grow out of narratives, that they are rooted in "the stories that people tell about themselves."[5] In this book we address the beliefs and practices that are necessary for us to develop cultures of peace. In various families and countries, we tell different stories. But as Christians, our beliefs and practices grow out of a profound, universal story—the story of God's grace and love which courses through the Hebrew Scriptures and the New Testament, climaxing in the incarnation, life and teaching, death and resurrection of Jesus Christ. This is the story which Peter (now part of a Jewish movement which claimed that Jesus was the Messiah) told to the Gentile soldier Cornelius, calling it the "good news of peace" (Acts 10:36). The culture of peace which our book describes grows out of many stories from many parts of the globe, but these stories are all judged by the same overarching narrative.

Finally, we have written about "cultures of peace" because the term "peace church" can sound parochial and private, as if it applied only to people from historic pacifist groups. We write from within the global Mennonite family, one of the historic peace churches, and many of our stories reflect Mennonite experience and struggles. But the "gospel of peace," from its first statement in Isaiah 52:7, was good news for *all* God's people. The gospel, and the practices of intercommunal peacemaking, worship, work, witness, and living in a world that is at war, belong to Christians of all traditions.

We have learned much from the thought and actions of Christians of many traditions; we rejoice to be a part of the church universal! We confess that we still have much to learn from other Christians. We have intended to root our book in the Bible story which unites us all and in the gospel which animates us all. As such, this book is an offering to the universal Church of Jesus Christ.

We pray that what you read here, the product of a collaboration of an Indonesian and two Americans, of a husband and wife and their friend, will be useful. All three of us have often heard that "peace brings problems" to a church. No doubt it does. But we sense intuitively that the gospel of peace, when integrated into all areas of the life and practice of the church, can bring life-changing benefits—a peace dividend! It takes imagination and hard work to learn the habits of peacemaking, and it is costly; true discipleship of Jesus always is costly. But it is worthwhile. No wonder both Testaments persistently talk about the "*good news* of peace!"

We believe that the rediscovery of peace will give new vitality to the life of the church. But what does this involve? The chapters that follow give both vision and a host of practical suggestions. Every chapter could be expanded greatly—we've just begun to deal with the challenge of being cultures of peace today. We invite you to add illustration and detail to these chapters as your church discovers the excitement of teaching and living both grace *and* peace.

"May the God of peace, who brought back from the dead our Lord Jesus . . . make you complete . . ." (Hebrews 13:20-21)—grace and peace!

Alan Kreider

Elkhart, Indiana, USA

Pentecost 2005

1.
The Church as a "Culture of Peace"

Should "peace" describe the Church's culture?

When someone says, "Tell me about your church," how do you respond? "It's near the supermarket." "Its worship is really meaningful, week after week." "Its members were helpful to me when I lost my job." "I can be real in my church, because people have been vulnerable with me."

Our experience of church may be less encouraging than that. "In our church things are tense." "There are groups that don't talk to each other." "There seems to be no connection between our worship and the real world."

Whether our experiences are positive or negative, it's unlikely that we will use the word *peace* to describe our church. We may feel peaceful when we go to church, but most of us probably wouldn't think of describing our church as being a "culture of peace."

But this is exactly how many Christians of the early centuries thought of their churches. Justin, a teacher who was martyred for his faith in Rome in the second century, stated an early Christian understanding; namely, that Isaiah 2:2-4, in which the prophet anticipates transforming swords into ploughshares, has been fulfilled in the church. Christians have come to Jesus to learn how to live. Justin reported about their experience:

> We . . . delighted in war, in the slaughter of one another, and in every other kind of iniquity; [but we] have in every part of the world converted our weapons of war into implements of peace—our swords into ploughshares, our spears into farmers' tools—and we *cultivate* piety, justice, brotherly charity, faith and hope, which we derive from the Father through the crucified Savior.[1]

Cultivating, for Justin, was creating a culture. Justin knew that God had done something new for the human race through sending the crucified Savior Jesus. God had caused people from many nations to gravitate to Jesus, who is the new Zion, and from him a new vision of life emerged. The result was a people of peace made up of former enemies. People of different tribes and nations, who used to hate each other, now shared life together. They dismantled the things that divided them and created a culture of justice, faith, and hope.

Justin knew that the life of the transnational church was proof that the Messiah Jesus had in fact brought peace which was already being experienced. Justin kept repeating: Isaiah 2:2-4 has been fulfilled in the church. People have been changed. They have converted their instruments of hostility so they might create a culture of peace. For Justin, as for Irenaeus, Tertullian, Origen, and other early Christian thinkers, God's peace, which Isaiah anticipated, has been realized through Christ. The church is evidence of this.[2]

Acts 10 and the origin of the church as a "culture of peace"

Where did Justin get this idea? From the church's beginnings in the book of Acts. In Acts the founding of the church was the product of God's peacemaking activity. Pentecost brought together Jews from many parts of the ancient world (Acts 2:9-11) who spoke many languages.

Pentecost transformed the linguistic chaos of Babel (Genesis 11:1-9) into peace and harmony. At Babel God had scattered people all over the world in chaos; on Pentecost God united people from all over the world into peace and harmony. At Babel God divided people into many groups separated from each other; on Pentecost God united people, who were previously separated, into one body. At Babel people could not understand each other because they suddenly spoke different languages; on Pentecost people from many languages could understand what other people spoke.

This did not mean that there were no tensions in the early Jerusalem church. Despite Pentecost, two distinct Jewish

cultural groupings persisted—the Hellenists and the Hebrews (Acts 6:1-6)—who experienced struggle as well as
unity in the Messiah Jesus.

But the big challenge for the early church lay in the relationship between Jews and Gentiles. The early Christians
claimed that in Christ Jesus, God had fulfilled his promise to
Abraham that he would bless all nations (Genesis 12:3). The
result was that Jews and their enemies—the Gentiles—could
be reconciled in a "bond of peace" (Ephesians 4:3). Getting
this started took a dramatic divine intervention, and the story of this intervention shows how central peace was to the
early Christians.

Acts 10 records the key events. They are so familiar that
they no longer surprise us. But how surprised Peter must
have been by them. Here he was in Caesarea (10:24ff). And
who was Peter? He was a Galilean Jew, whose friend Jesus had
recently been crucified as a criminal by the Roman occupation
forces. And where was Peter? He was in a dangerous place for
Jews. As the headquarters of Roman power in Palestine, Caesarea was full of soldiers and violence. As a pagan city, it was
full of Gentiles, idols, and non-kosher food. Peter and his
companions were Jews, friends of a crucified man, among
their enemies. They were among Gentiles who were oppress-
ing their country, exploiting it, and tampering with their worship in the temple. Peter and his friends could never have expected to find themselves in the house of a Roman officer like
Cornelius.

But God was at work in the enemy's house in Caesarea. And this was where things clicked for Peter. Peter listened to Cornelius and thought again about the visions that God had given him of clean and unclean food.

Peter learned through these visions that religious laws created by religious tradition could not stop God from doing his reconciling work. Peter knew that, according to the Jewish laws, a Jew was prohibited from associating with Gentiles or visiting with them. But God had shown him that such laws no longer had meaning and that the barrier was no longer relevant (10:28). Since the coming of Jesus Christ, the Prince of Peace, the old pattern of reconciliation had been turned upside down. In the old tradition, reconciliation had to come first, before acceptance. Hence, people were required to bring offerings to God first, before reconciliation; only then could God accept people in his embrace. But Jesus demonstrated over and over again that acceptance precedes reconciliation. It was God's acceptance of Cornelius that opened Peter's eyes and brought him towards reconciliation. As God had done in accepting Cornelius, so God called Peter to do.

Peter then had an "aha" experience. He said, "I truly understand that God shows no partiality" (10:34). This is a Jew speaking! No longer will there be insiders and outsiders, clean Jews and unclean Gentiles, divided by an unbreachable wall. God has a big design. Because of the work of Jesus Christ which the Holy Spirit has ratified, God's people will

no longer just be the Jews. They will be people of every nation—Jews *and* Gentiles.

Imagine how rapidly Peter was thinking, how deeply he
was praying, as he tried to make sense of all this. His instinct
was to think—and to tell Cornelius—about Jesus (10:36ff).
God, said Peter, had sent a message, brought by the Messiah
Jesus, who "announced the good news of peace" (the Greek
text says that Jesus "evangelized peace"). Here Peter was
talking about peace to an occupation soldier. The Roman
empire said that "Caesar is Lord," but Peter, in the Roman
garrison, claimed that Jesus, not Caesar, is "Lord of all." Peter went on to tell Cornelius the outlines of Jesus' life, death,
and resurrection. And the result of this was that there can be
forgiveness and inclusion for *everyone*—insider and outsider—who fears God and does justice (10:35).

What might Jesus have had in mind as he announced the
"good news of peace"? Peter must have pondered this. Peter
would have thought about Old Testament prophecies, especially Isaiah 52:7 which anticipated the "messenger who an-
nounces peace"; he would have remembered that this passage
was especially dear to Jesus.[3] Peter would also have thought
about Jesus' life. Jesus had taught about God's grand design,
not just for Jews, but for people from all nations. Jesus had associated with sinners and outsiders, children and women,
even enemy soldiers; he had brought unlikely people together.
In doing these things he had threatened vested interests; he
had come, he said, "not to bring peace but division" (Luke

12:51; see also Matthew 10:34). Because he shook people's prejudices and acted with sovereign truth, Jesus made enemies. They plotted against him and crucified him.

But Jesus had always offered people another way. It was a more radical way of dealing with the political crisis in Palestine than anyone had imagined—by bringing Romans alongside Jews in God's family of forgiveness and reconciliation. Both Matthew and Luke record that *Jesus gave prominent place to teaching about enemies:* in Matthew 5:43ff, this teaching comes as the climax of the "antitheses" of the Sermon on the Mount; in Luke 6:27ff, it comes as Jesus' first ethical teaching. And in both, the message is the same. "Love your enemies; pray for them," he said.

Jesus himself had received a national enemy, a Roman centurion, marveled at his faith, and looked forward to the time when people from the East and the West would join with the lineal descendants of Abraham at a table in God's Kingdom (Matthew 8:11).

Jesus' way was controversial. It was incomprehensible to some and threatening to others. As Jesus looked over Jerusalem (Luke 19:41ff), he wept because the people did not know "the things that make for peace." People were rejecting his announcement of the good news of peace. So Jesus predicted that "their enemies" the Romans would come, erect siege engines around Jerusalem, smash the city, and crush its children. Some years later, in the Jewish War of 66-70, AD, this happened. With great brutality the Romans destroyed Jerusalem and its temple, killing countless people and beginning a crisis of Jewish identity.

But here, in enemy Caesarea, on the Gentile fringes of the Jewish world, something new was happening. Peter asserts: Jesus Christ, in his death on a Roman cross, has forgiven the sins of his enemies and made peace. And that's not the end of it: in the resurrection, God has declared his son to be "Lord of all" (Acts 10:36). God vindicated the foolishness of his peacemaking Son. By so doing, God declared that the way of peace which his Son, Jesus Christ, had demonstrated is the true way of life. As Peter was speaking, the Holy Spirit gave a loud "Amen," pouring out upon the outsiders the same spiritual gifts as those which the insiders had experienced (Acts 10:44). Because of the work of God in Christ and the active reality of the Holy Spirit, peace is possible between estranged humans.

So in Caesarea, Peter was doing what Jesus had wanted. Led by the Holy Spirit, Peter was making peace with a Roman. The nations of Peter and Cornelius were heading for war. But in the Messiah Jesus they were standing together as brothers.

Peter and Cornelius are the nucleus of a new transnational people of peace. In the future, God's family will be multicultural, multi-ethnic. It will be drawn from those in every nation who "fear God and do justice"—and who are open to God's forgiving and reconciling work. This family will be a household of peace in which unreconciled enemies are reconciled, in which unforgiven people are forgiven, and in which they are given a common mission—to share the "good news of peace" with all nations.

We would like to know what happened next! Did Cornelius stay in the army or did he leave it? What did his friends and relatives do? We don't know. We do know a bit more about Peter's future. He had to defend his unprecedented actions to the church leaders in Jerusalem (Acts 11:1-18). Later he went to Rome where he helped to build a multi-ethnic church and was crucified, according to accounts, upside down.[4]

This event in Caesarea was not a high-profile news story. It was obscure, hidden, as truly significant developments often are. But it was a breakthrough moment in the history of the church. This is where we—all Christians who do not have Jewish parents—enter the story. Cornelius, the enemy outsider whom God made a brother through the peacemaking work of Christ, is our forerunner. Isn't it fascinating that God chose a soldier, an enemy soldier, to play this role?

What began in Caesarea was very important. That's why it's not surprising that the New Testament writers developed a messianic culture of peace that is in harmony with what God did, and what Peter said, in Caesarea. This culture is both theological and practical. We will turn to this culture of peace in our second chapter.

2.
Peace in the New Testament:
A Jewel with Many Facets

The story of Peter and Cornelius in Acts 10 is a breakthrough. The story is also illuminating. It shows us God at work, doing what is so important to God—making peace. In this story we can see many facets of God's peacemaking work. These facets are so important that other New Testament writers deal with them, too.

Peace is central to God's work and will

This was clear to Peter as he spoke to Cornelius in Acts 10. It is evident in the way he presented Jesus: "He came evangelizing peace" (10:36, alluding to Isaiah 52:7). It is also clear in the way Peter responded when he found that God was at work in the wrong person—the enemy. And it is central throughout the New Testament. Why was peace so important to the early Christians? Because they, with gratitude and puzzlement, were trying to come to terms with what God had done. Through the work of Christ and the power of the Holy Spirit, God had made them, despite their different races and backgrounds, into one body. They knew what later Christians have found easy to forget: our origins, as the church of Jesus Christ, are in miraculous reconciliation.

How do the New Testament writers present the central place of peace in God's work and will? They do this by the words that they use and the theology they develop.

Words. Repeatedly the New Testament Christians call God "the God of peace." Routinely they refer to the good news as "the gospel of peace."[1] In the New Testament—as in the Hebrew Scriptures—peace is literally all over the place. God has justified us by faith and has given us peace with God; through the work of Christ on the cross, God has made peace between us and God (Romans 5:1, 10). God has called us to peace (1 Corinthians 7:15); we are to know "the peace of God, which surpasses all understanding" (Philippians 4:7). Two New Testament authors urge their friends to "seek peace with everyone" (Hebrews 12:14; 1 Peter 3:11). In letter after letter, Paul, like Peter and John, begins with the expression "grace to you and peace"—a potent coupling.

Theology. In chapter 2 of his letter to the Christians in Ephesus, Paul deals with grace and peace, presenting them as in-

terlocking, interdependent, essential New Testament themes.
Let's paraphrase verses 11-22, listening to them as if we
were Cornelius, an outsider, a Gentile.

"Remember, Cornelius, you Gentiles were not like us
Jewish insiders. You were outsiders. You were aliens from
the commonwealth of Israel; you were strangers, without
God and without hope [verses11-12]. But by the blood of
Christ you Gentile outsiders have been brought near. Jesus
is our peace. He has broken down the wall dividing insiders
from outsiders. Jesus has ended the hostility. Jesus has evangelized peace [v. 17—the same expression as Acts 10:36] to
outsiders as well as insiders. And he has died on the Cross,
giving his life for others, reconciling us all, both us Jewish
insiders and you Gentile outsiders, to God [verse 16]. By
grace, God has done the impossible; through Jesus, God has
broken down the wall of hostility dividing you Gentile outsiders from us Jewish insiders; and through the broken wall
'one new humanity' has come into being, made up of former
enemies. This new humanity is the church, the household of
God. This, Cornelius, is what 'making peace' is all about
[verse 15]. It's not like the Roman peace (Pax Romana); it's
much more profound than that. It is the peace of Christ (Pax
Christi), in which former enemies are reconciled to God and
become brothers and sisters in God's family."

So Cornelius, like the Christians in Ephesus, would have
known that the church, wherever it was found, was a peace

church. God had broken down the wall, the wall that separated, stereotyped, and prevented communion.

In Christ, God is at work creating a new humanity. Christ is our peace. So in the church in Ephesus, peace was not an optional concern of some of its members. No, in Ephesus there was a *culture of peace* in which peace was important to all members. Why? Because the peace that they knew was rooted in their fundamental experience as Christians of forgiveness and reconciliation in Christ. Peace, now as well as then, is central to God's work and will.

Peace is at the heart of God's mission

Think about Peter and Cornelius on their breakthrough day in Caesarea. Wouldn't God's remarkable action, ratified by the Holy Spirit, have made it perfectly clear to them that peace is central to God's mission?

In Caesarea in Acts 10 God was at work. For Jews, Caesarea was a repulsive place—a Roman garrison city. It was the center of Roman military power. The Roman soldiers were occupation troops, battle-hardened, unlikely people to be instruments of God's work. But in God's sight no human can be called unreachable. There may be people whom we fellow humans are unable to reach. But these people are certainly not beyond God's reach. Before Peter met Cornelius, God had already gone ahead of him and reached Cornelius. Peter only followed the path God had pioneered. Peter had no mission of his own. His mission was God's mission.

It was in Caesarea that God was doing something surprising, stirring the hearts of the enemy, giving them a desire to know God, and, as a result, calling Jewish believers like Peter to change their worldview and priorities. God was at work in Caesarea, and God's work required everybody to change. On the margins, in obscurity, in a place of danger and risk, God was initiating something small that would become huge—the global church.

Here, and in the rest of the New Testament, God's mission is massive. In Matthew 8:11, Jesus saw God at work in another centurion and looked forward to the day when "many will come from the east and west and will eat with Abraham and Isaac and Jacob in the Kingdom of heaven." In Revelation 7:9, the revelator John saw "a great multitude that no one could count, from every nation, from all tribes and peoples and languages" who were worshipping Jesus the Lamb. God's mission, in the New Testament and beyond, is to bring this about—"one new humanity," together eating in peace, together worshipping the Lamb.

From the beginning this has been God's mission. But people weren't always clear what this meant. The believers in the early Christian congregations knew that Christ had made peace and had reconciled them to God and to people who were unlike them. Wonderful! But what did this mean for their churches?

In his visits and letters, Paul struggled to advise and encourage communities of ordinary people who were doing something extraordinary—bringing former enemies (Jews and Gentiles) together. This wasn't easy; it created problems. What kinds of food should they eat? On what day of the week should they meet? What approaches should they take to marriage, to law courts, to Jewish customs? The Council of Jerusalem in Acts 15 was an important attempt, by the leaders of the early churches, to deal with the conflicts that were inevitable as they sought to become a new humanity, a people of peace. And note who was the crucial witness in the discussions in Jerusalem. It was Peter, testifying to what God had done in Caesarea (Acts 15:7-11).

How had Peter responded to what he saw God doing in Caesarea? When he saw that God was giving the Holy Spirit to the enemy Gentiles, as God had given to Jesus' Jewish disciples, Peter flowed with God—he baptized the enemy (Acts 10:47). When he defended his action to the elders in Jerusalem, his defense was that it was God who was responsible: "Who was I that I could hinder God?" (Acts 11:17). In Acts 15, at the Council in Jerusalem, Peter was inviting the Jerusalem leaders to do as he had done in Caesarea—to flow with what God was doing. And this is what God calls us today to do: to see where God is at work and to be co-workers with God. Jesus had said, "The Son can do nothing on his own, but only what he sees the Father doing" (John 5:19).

Today God's mission is still a peacemaking mission. The global church of the twenty-first century is an amazing expression of this. In the twentieth century, Christianity's

heartlands moved South, to the Southern continents. So the
church in the twenty-first century is made up of Peters and
Corneliuses—former enemies, former slaves and former
masters, former colonizers and former revolutionaries, former oppressors and formerly oppressed.[2] God has been
breaking down the walls—forgiving us all, reconciling us all
to God, imparting to us all the peace of Christ, making us all
members of an international communion of peace.

The global Christian church is a miracle. It is a new family. It gives us our primary identity, a place where we by
God's grace can know who we are and can know where we
really belong. God is doing this globally today. Our calling
today is like that of Peter's—not to "hinder God" (Acts
11:17), not to get in God's way, but to enter into God's mission of making peace.

Peace is a response to God's grace

In Acts 10, Peter and Cornelius were not hunting a new vision for humanity. Peter's immediate concern was lunch—
"He became hungry and wanted something to eat" (10:10);
his larger concern was to help a Jewish messianic renewal
movement to grow and flourish. Cornelius's goals were similarly modest: he was trying to be a god-fearer, to worship the
God of the Jews as best he could while being a Roman soldier.

But God was going ahead of Peter and Cornelius. God was
graciously expanding their horizons. What happened was
not something that Peter and Cornelius planned. It was not

something that they engineered. No, what happened was the gift of the gracious God. God's vision was bigger than theirs; God's work was ahead of theirs. So God forgave Peter and Cornelius, reconciled them, and gave them a new vision and a new identity. All this was because God is gracious.

This is the way it always is. God's grace comes first, and then God invites humans to respond. It is a mistake to understand God's grace simply in terms of justification, as if God does everything and humans do nothing. God's grace delivers, empowers, and sanctifies. It delivers humans from the bondage of separation and isolation. Grace empowers humans to be reconciled with former enemies. It sanctifies humans to become peacemakers. And it is for us to respond to such a grace. No one, not even God, can force us to respond to God's grace. The response must be born out of our freedom. German theologian Dietrich Bonhoeffer once said that responsible action is a "free venture" because it is we, the agents, "who must observe, judge, weigh up, decide, and act."[3]

Thus, the miracle of God's grace flows when humans respond to God's question, "Where are you?" (Genesis 3:9), with their question, "Where is the child?" (Matthew 2:2). It is no coincidence that our Scriptures are framed by these two theological questions; the first opens the Old Testament, the second the New Testament.

As the Bible's story unfolds, God searches for humans who live in sin, and humans respond, seeking the God who alone can provide true salvation. God acts first, in ways that can be astonishing and moving, and God's acts elicit our worship and praise. God then asks us humans to respond by changing our minds, our lives, our priorities. The miracle of God's grace is that we no longer orient our lives to ourselves but to God, so that we can proclaim just as the apostle Paul did, "It is no longer I who live, but it is Christ who lives in me" (Galatians 2:20). Each aspect of our experience of God has a consequence. God's grace is free, but it requires a response.

- God has forgiven us; therefore we are to become a people whose lives are marked by forgiveness. "Forgive us our sins, as we forgive those who sin against us" (Matthew 6:12).
- God has reconciled us to God; therefore we are to be reconciled with our enemies, and we are given a ministry of reconciliation (2 Corinthians 5:18).
- God has given us God's peace; therefore we are to be peacemakers. "Blessed are the peacemakers, for they shall be called God's children" (Matthew 5:10).

Theologian Miroslav Volf has put it like this:

> Inscribed on the very heart of God's grace is the rule that we can be its recipients only if we do not resist being made into its agents; what happens to us must be done by us.[4]

Peter and Cornelius in Acts 10 were recipients of grace; God, the gracious one, called them to be agents of grace.

And this meant making peace. It meant becoming collaborators with God as God made grace and peace in the lives of many people. It meant changing their worldview, their view of the enemy, their priorities. It meant taking risks. If they wanted to know the grace of God, they were called to be peacemakers. Likewise, for us: if we want to know the grace of God, we must be agents of God's grace and peace.

Peace is big: the word peace

In Acts 10:36 Peter told Cornelius, "Jesus came evangelizing peace." But what does peace mean?

The peace to which the peace church is called is big. In everyday life we often use the word "peace" in ways that don't help us understand what peace means in the Bible: "I wish the neighbors would turn down their music and give me some peace"; "Thanks to the Bomb we've had 40 years of peace in Europe." Occasionally we use a word that we view as an equivalent to peace—"nonviolence."

Here are four approaches to thinking about peace:

- *Peace as a negative.* For example, "There is no war, so this must be peace." This is superficial. It feeds on personal feelings and individual experience and takes a narrow perspective.
- *Peace as things that support peace.* For example we might say, "There are people working for the suppression and termination of all kinds of oppression in society and of individual, as well as structural, violence."[5]

- *Peace with a focus: peace is necessary to terminate all violence.* This approach perceives violence as the main barrier to peace.
- *Peace as transformation of conflict.* The focus here is not on the violence, but on the conflict. In this approach, to understand peace we have to understand the anatomy and mechanism of conflict and how conflict can be transformed creatively and nonviolently.[6]

Peace in the Bible is of all this, but more. Biblical scholars remind us that the Hebrew word *shalom*, often translated "peace," appears 235 times in the Old Testament[7] and refers to many things in various contexts. *Shalom* provides the concept of peace behind the New Testament word *eirene*.

Biblical peace, *shalom*, refers first of all to *well-being* and *material prosperity*, signified by the presence of physical well-being and the absence of the threat of war, disease, or famine (Jeremiah 33:6, 9). Second, peace refers to *just relationships* signified by right relations between people and between nations, as well as to social order and harmony in which there is no oppression or exclusion in any form (Isaiah 54:13-14). Third, peace also refers to the *moral integrity* of a person in whom there is straightforwardness and no deceit, fault, or blame (Psalm 34:13-14). In the New Testament, peace, *eirene*, receives yet another nuance. It is related to God and the good news from God. Notice the expression "the God of peace" (Romans 15:33; 16.20; 2 Corinthians 13:11; 1 Thessalonians 5:23; 2 Thessalonians 3:16; Hebrews 13:20).[8]

Peace in the Bible is related to the *wholeness,* an all-embracing wholeness, of humans and all creation.[9] It involves the *physical, relational, moral,* as well as *spiritual,* dimensions of humankind. Peter knew this. As he declared the "good news of peace" to Cornelius, he said that in every nation people would be acceptable to God who "fear God and do justice" (Acts 10:35). Justice, Peter knew, was a precondition for *shalom;* "the effect of justice will be *shalom*" (Isaiah 32.17). To Peter's Jewish way of thinking, there can be no peace when relationships are broken, when people are out of harmony with God and with each other, when injustice and hatred and fear prevail. So Peter and Cornelius were moving toward a big vision of peace, in which God will "put together a broken world."[10]

The same was true of the early church. Justin Martyr said that Christians through the work of the crucified Savior had converted their weapons of war into peaceful farming tools. And what did they cultivate? "Piety, justice, brotherly charity, faith, and hope."[11] Peace, as Jesus and Peter and the early Christians evangelized it, was big and beautiful. It involved justice and a transformation of broken and oppressive relationships in a culture of peace.

Peace is personal and interpersonal

Peter spoke about peace; he and Cornelius and the many people gathered in the garrison in Caesarea experienced peace. This peace/*shalom*/*eirene* was infinitely personal—God's rec-

onciling, forgiving, loving work. God through the work of
Christ and the moving of the Holy Spirit was forgiving people
their sins and reconciling them to himself (Acts 10:43). So Peter asked, "Can anyone withhold the water for baptizing these
people [Gentiles]?" (Acts 10:47). This question was a challenging one. For baptism, then as now, was a means of incor-
porating people into a new family who would become brothers and sisters in Christ. The act of baptism was eloquent. It
said that people who had been reconciled to God could now
live in peace with others, including their former enemies.

Peace—the biblical peace of *shalom* and *eirene*—was an expression of God's healing work which was both personal and
corporate. The New Testament writers knew what Peter and
Cornelius celebrated together: God's peace reconciles people
to God; it restores relationships between humans; it brings
enemies together into a new social reality.

In Indonesia today, one way to identify people is by dif-
ferentiating between those of Chinese descent and the so-
called indigenous people. But Indonesian Christians find a
new identity. I (Paulus) was born into a Chinese family. As
an Indonesian of Chinese descent, I have experienced discrimination all my life. People have treated me as a person of
no worth. I recall that, when I was a kid, my indigenous
neighbors often stopped me while I was riding to school on
my bicycle. They asked me for money. If I gave them money,
I would be okay. But if I did not give them money, they
would beat me up on the street. They also liked to shout

"Chinese! Chinese!" at me as I was passing by, which in the Indonesian context was very humiliating. Often as they shouted they threw gravel at me. Sometimes they even threw firecrackers. As I grew up, I found out that there was a code number on my ID card which enabled public officers to identify my Chinese background. Because I had that code, I was not free to enter public schools or work in public offices. That was my situation in society.

I grew up wondering why my indigenous neighbors could not accept me simply as a human being. Why did they despise me? However, when I joined the church, I found that my Chinese identity was is not as important as my Christian identity. Now there was neither Jew nor Greek, neither Chinese nor indigenous (Galatians 3:28). All Christians share a new and common identity, and therefore we are all equals. Or, a better way to say it is that there are now Chinese Christians and indigenous Christians, and the name "Christian" is all that matters.

In his book *Social Sources of Denominationalism,* H. Richard Niebuhr argues that the true church is a church "which has transcended the divisions of the world."[12] This is what Peter and Cornelius discovered. Such a church is a sign to the world that its brokenness can be healed.[13]

Peace is a continuum

On one end of the continuum there is "peace with God" (Romans 5.1), which results from God's act of justifying us and making our relationship with him right and open. At the other end there is peace between people and nations, resulting from God's building of reconciled relationships between former enemies. Here are two ways of thinking about the continuum.

The ripple effect. A pastor of a Mennonite Brethren church in Wichita, Kansas, USA, teaches people who come to classes for new church members: "The most important question is: Have you made peace with God?" If they have, the pastor tells them, "Peace then ripples out and begins to affect all our other circles of relationship"—including relationships in the family, in the workplace, and with one's enemies. The pastor encourages the ripple, urging these people who are at peace with God to participate in God's peacemaking in new places, including their relationship with their nation's enemies, so that God's peace may be comprehensive. [14]

At one end of the continuum, according to the *ripple effect,* is our peace with God. Peacemaking always starts with peace with God. Without peace with God we cannot speak about peacemaking, let alone to do it. Peace always starts from within and then moves outward. It originates in a peaceful relationship between God, the source of peace, and us. But God who is the source of peace also wills peace for all his creation. God does not want us to stay in the first stage. He wants us to move forward to the next stages on the continuum—peace with ourselves, peace with our neighbors, peace with our fellow citizens, and, in the end, peace with our enemies. We can see this will of God very clearly in Jesus Christ who demonstrated the way of peace through his life and ministry. In Christ we see the risk and hope, as well as the joy, of that way of life.

At one end of the continuum there is peace with God; at the other end we find peace with our *enemies*, the stage most difficult to achieve. We may know peace with God, but we may not be in peace with our enemies, particularly with those who have hurt us physically or emotionally. This explains why Christians who have been involved in bloody conflicts, such as those in Indonesia, Northern Ireland, or Congo, find it difficult to reconcile themselves with people whom they perceive as their enemies. This, however, should not discourage us, nor should it become a barrier for us to get involved in peacemaking.

Between the two ends of the continuum—peace with God and peace with enemies—there are many expressions of peace. We may not be ready yet to make peace with our enemies, but that does not mean that we are excluded from peacemaking. There are many kinds of peacemaking which we can be involved in, including peace within, peace with our families (nuclear and extended), peace with our sisters and brothers in Christ in the local church, peace with our sisters and brothers in Christ in other churches, peace with people of other faiths, peace with our neighbors, peace with our colleagues at work, peace with other citizens within our nation, peace with citizens of other countries.

God is at work. This approach is slightly different from the *ripple effect.* This is being aware that the God who revealed himself in Jesus Christ is making *shalom* in many ways. At times God is working in the heart of Cornelius, the enemy centurion, before he knows God. At times God is using the ecologist who is seeking the *shalom* of creation. At times God is granting forgiveness and peace to individuals who are alienated from God. According to this understanding, God's peacemaking action may not always *start* with the forgiveness of an individual, but God desires that his peacemaking action always include this. God's purpose is to move history towards a peace that is comprehensive (Isaiah 11:1-9). As Paul put it (2 Thessalonians 3:16), "The Lord of peace [will] give you peace at all times in all ways."

God's peace is big. It is all-embracing. It is both personal and interpersonal. It restores relationships between us and God, between us and our enemies, between us and God's creation. It can be experienced already, as an anticipation of what God wants everyone to experience. Already, in Christ, Peter and Cornelius were learning to live as everyone will someday live. Today, we, too, experience the reality of God's personal and interpersonal peacemaking in the transnational community of peace which is called the Church. God calls the Church to embrace a big vision of peace, with every member a peacemaker.

Peace has to be made

Peace is made painfully. What God was beginning with Peter and Cornelius had to be worked out. In Caesarea, peace with God could be declared, and peace between Jews and Gentiles could be celebrated. But then problems occurred and conflict broke out. Relating to the Roman Gentiles got Peter in trouble with the church leaders in Jerusalem: "Why did you go to uncircumcised men and eat with them?" (Acts 11:3).

Peace has to be made because the world is full of broken relationships and injustice. God invites us to share in his peacemaking work and way. "Blessed are the peace*makers*, because they shall be called God's children" (Matthew 5:9). Until God's Kingdom comes in fullness, peace will never be complete. It always has to be made. Jesus' uncle Zechariah ended his song in Luke 1:78-79 by celebrating "the tender mercy of our God" who is committed "to give light to those who sit in darkness and the shadow of death, to guide our feet into the way of peace." In a world of conflict, there is no way to peace; peace itself is the way. Becoming people of peace requires a struggle between our God-given freedom and our human, finite limitations.

Jesus proclaimed the good news of peace. He blessed peacemakers; he practiced peacemaking. And he recognized that this involved conflict. Jesus was explicit about this; he came to bring not peace but a sword (Matthew 10:34). Without conflict, injustice is fixed and unchallenged, and there is no hope.

So Jesus entered into the conflict that makes peace: he set his face to Jerusalem; he caused an uproar in the Temple, the heart of his nation's religious establishment; he out-thought the religious leaders. And he paid the price: the cross is central to Christ's peacemaking work. The cross is the product of his peacemaking; it also, New Testament writers emphasize repeatedly, is the means of his peacemaking. Christ has made "peace through the blood of his cross" (Colossians 1:20, echoing Isaiah 53:5). A church that is becoming a culture of peace ponders Christ's cross-oriented life and his saving work on the cross, and it opens itself to take up its cross. As it does so, God leads it into the adventure, risk, and suffering of peacemaking conflict.

Peace leads to surprise

In the ancient world, few things would have been more surprising than what happened in Acts 10. Galileans like Peter, who were friends of a man crucified by the Romans, did not expect to visit a centurion's house in Caesarea. To most observers, the idea of a "new humanity," bringing together Romans and Jews in a global messianic family, was intensely surprising. It seemed a strange mingling of incompatible communities, not a creative new solution to an intractable problem. How odd, how surprising, these messianic nonconformists were who believed that through Christ the enemy had become a brother. Those who claimed that this had happened because of "the cross," in which curse mingled with cruelty, risked being dismissed as foolish, unrealistic, and uncouth.

So instead of facing into surprise, many Jewish people chose to prepare themselves for something more comprehensible—revolutionary war against the Romans. This took place between 66 and 70 A.D., with tragic consequences for the Jewish people—the scattering of the people of Jerusalem and the destruction of the temple. God had another way, which was to bring about a global family in Christ made up of former enemies. God is still doing this, thinking bigger than our stereotypes, bringing about a church—a "holy nation"—which is global. God is the God of surprises. God surprised Peter, who decided that he would no longer think or act as a typical first-century Jew. The peacemaking God continues to surprise.

Peace is made through God's power

Peter said to Cornelius (Acts 10:39-40), "They put Jesus to death by hanging him on a tree, but God raised him." The peacemaking work of God is manifested in resurrection. The resurrection of Jesus shows God's determination to ratify the way of peace. An early Christian blessing said, "May the God of peace, who brought back from the dead our Lord Jesus . . ." (Hebrews 13:20). Death cannot stop the peacemaking God. Impossibility cannot stop the peacemaking God. As Paul wrote to the Romans (Romans 4:17), God "gives life to the dead and calls into existence the things that do not exist." For humans in their own strength, peace is impossible; peacemaking is what God does. So, by God's grace, in the 1990s in South Africa there was no race war, but, miraculously, a "Truth and Reconciliation Commission." God's power, collaborating with people's prayers and courage, brings about change. In our twenty-first-century world as in first-century Caesarea, the Holy Spirit is the midwife of new possibilities. The Spirit falls on Romans, on oppressors, on enemies, on the weak, and on those asked to do humanly impossible things. It is only because of resurrection and the Holy Spirit that God's people can be peacemakers.

Jesus is the key to peace

Peace, Peter told Cornelius, was what Jesus evangelized (Acts 10:36). Ephesians 2:14 says of Jesus, "He is our peace." Jesus is the peacemaker. To know what peace means, we don't argue politics or theology; we look at Jesus. We tell the story of Jesus. We listen to Jesus. We watch Jesus in action—Jesus with his friends, Jesus in conflict, Jesus loving his enemies, Jesus on the cross, Jesus making peace. The church's task, from generation to generation, is to ponder the story and teachings of Jesus and to pass on Jesus' ways. Paul saw his task in this light—to invite people to "be imitators of me as I am of Christ" (1 Corinthians 11:1). Jesus' ways, lived by his followers, would become ways to be lived—and copied—by others. As Paul said to the Christians in Philippi, "Keep on doing the things you have learned and received and heard and seen in me, and the God of peace will be with you" (Philippians 4:9). Jesus, the embodiment of the peace of God, is alive. Paul says, "He himself is our peace," and he shows us what peace is all about.

Peace is central to biblical faith. It is impossible to exaggerate this. All eight of these facets indicate that, in the Bible, peace is not an extra-cost option. It is central. The only reason that we Gentiles (Indonesian Gentiles, Argentinian Gentiles, Canadian Gentiles, and all the rest) are in the church is God's miraculous act of peacemaking in Christ. So peace is for the whole church. In fact, peace is a word that we could use to designate our churches. When people ask us, "Tell me about your church," we could say, "We're a culture of peace. God is a God of peace, and we're learning what peace means. It's exciting. Would you like to come and see?"

3.
Does Peace Work?

Finding peace and celebrating it

The God of the Bible is the "God of peace" (Judges 6:24; 1 Thessalonians 5:23; Hebrews 13:20; etc). All of us know churches in which God's peacemaking work is evident. It is a useful discipline to ask each other, in our own congregations and when gathering together with other Christians, "Where have you seen God making peace recently?"

The Peace Council of Mennonite World Conference asked member conferences to report where they had recently experienced God's peacemaking. Although these stories are confined to this particular Christian denomination, their stories show many points on the peacemaking continuum.

Personal stories. A church in Nicaragua reported the story of Margarita, who in a conversion experience came to know the peace of God. Margarita was an abused and oppressed woman, abandoned by her lovers. To support her sons she had to work constantly for low wages. She was violent, given to "arguments, fights, and quarrels with her neighbors." People denounced her to the police as "an undesirable neighbor." But when Margarita took Jesus into her heart, "her whole life changed for the better for herself and her neighbors, who couldn't get over their surprise at the change in her life." Margarita no longer mistreats her sons. And her neighbors, who had feared her, have come to admire her. The Nicaraguan Mennonites report, "Our God is the God of the impossible, who does things that no one can believe."[1]

Stories of peacemaking within churches. The Evangelical Mennonite Community, Congo (CEM), was torn apart by internal strife which, they realized, was hindering their witness. They report that they were not able to initiate "any outreach activities, because we have needed to establish peace within our own conference." In humility they turned to a "peace and reconciliation commission," which mediated between the conference's presidency and its oversight committee. This mediation led to resolution, for which they praise God. The conflict has led them to affirm that "Reconciliation is our mission" and to seek training in the disciplines and skills of peacemaking.[2]

Stories of peacemaking with neighbors. In India, the Bihar Mennonite Mandali experienced tension with the Maoist Communist Center, a group of revolutionaries who had committed acts of violence and murder. The Bihar Mennonites report that Peter Minj, a Bihar Mennonite leader, told the Maoist leaders, "We Mennonites will never take part in shedding blood or other evil works of your group." But he indicated to them that the Mennonites wanted to remain in contact with the Maoists. The report stated that the Mennonites have been "praying and waiting for that day when these people will fall at the feet of Jesus." And it noted changes in their enemies. Some Maoists have been willing to give up the way of violence. And those who remain active as Maoists have come to trust the Mennonites. When a church leader recently got lost and strayed into unfamiliar territory, a Maoist group abducted him and threatened to kill him. But when they learned that he was a Mennonite, "their behavior suddenly changed." The Maoists' approach became respectful, and they "invited him for a cup of tea," because, the Bihar Mennonites reported, "people of the area know that we Mennonites are very loving to all and we sincerely try to do good to them." With the Maoists, whom their nation views as enemies, the Bihar Mennonites remain at peace.[3]

Stories of peacemaking with people of other faiths. Indonesia has the largest Islamic population of any country, and, in parts of Indonesia, Christian churches have been burned, and there have been outbreaks of killing. In this setting, Mennonite Christians of the GKMI synod have worked together with Catholic and Protestant Christians and have also engaged Islamic leaders in dialogue. In the town of Solo, well-known for centuries for religious and ethnic conflicts, Christian pastors and Muslim Imams have formed an interfaith forum which has sought to oppose communal violence. The forum's aim has been "to install peace values in communal ties." This has led to symbolic events, such as the occasion in which the Mennonites distributed 3000 T-shirts to members of many religious groups. On the T-shirts were the words, "I'm a Member of a Peace-Loving Community." The forum has gone even further. In five districts of the city they have established "community mediation groups," each consisting of about 20 trained mediators, representing each of the religions, to function as mediators when there is community conflict.[4]

Stories of peacemaking between nations. The CMCO conference of Mennonites in Congo reports that in their country "intermittent wars and other conflicts . . . have destroyed fragile interpersonal relationships, as well as international relationships among the Great Lakes countries . . ." Congolese Mennonite Christians recognized that their mission, "as salt and light in the world," is to "re-establish broken relationships between individuals and nations." So they have functioned as active participants in the Inter-Congolese Dialogue of Reconciliation, which has attempted to bring peace between warring groups in the Congo.

Congolese Mennonites also participated in a group working for peace between nations (DR Congo, Uganda, Rwanda, and Burundi) which have been at war in the Great Lakes region in central Africa. Even in the midst of war, the Congolese affirm, "Christ is our peace. He gives us peace, his peace . . ." His followers will be "active builders of peace in their personal lives as well as in their ministry and society . . . their only method of work will be one of nonviolence."[5]

These stories are illustrations of something huge. Since God is the God of peace, it's not surprising that God is making peace all the time, in many places by many kinds of people in every area of human experience. We need to increase the number of these stories, not least by reflecting on our own lives and recalling ways in which God has used us as peacemakers. The Bible shows us that God also uses people who do not know him to serve him by making peace. We need to recognize these things, learn from them, and praise God for them.

Why some people have reservations about peace

But very few churches call themselves cultures of peace. Christians, it appears, are more comfortable with the label "grace" than "peace"—even though Paul and Peter began their letters by holding them together. Christians also seem to have difficulty talking about the peacemaking that God is doing within the Church and beyond it. At times our churches are characterized by broken relationships, power-plays, and manipulation. In these churches it is understandable why people talk so little about peace. Even some healthy churches rarely talk about peace. If a member seeks to put peace on the agenda it may be treated as strange, beside the point, or unwelcome.

Why? It is important for us to listen to reasons for which Christians have distanced themselves from talk about peace. Some explanations that we have heard are:

- *"Peace will dilute the gospel."* It will divert attention from evangelism.
- *"Peace will bring politics into the church."* Politics brings conflict, and many Christians have had bad experience with conflict. They don't know how to deal with it, and so they try to avoid admitting conflict.
- *"Peace sounds like 'pacifism.'"* To some Christians, pacifism has a bad feel. Some Christians view it as too activist— "peace with a fist." Other Christians view pacifism as too passive. They believe that human experience shows that it is necessary for Christians to resist tyrants. After all, Americans and the British say, "What if we hadn't stood up to Hitler?"
- *"Talking about peace belittles our experience and suffering in war."* Christians, including Mennonite Christians, have fought in wars; they have killed and been killed; the survivors have suffered post-battle trauma; they have lost relatives in wars. These people don't like it when other Christians who talk of peace seem to demean their experiences in war. Further, some people have experienced good things in the military: "I was converted in the Navy"; "I'm so grateful for the Army, which gave me the chance at an education."

- *"Peace is boring."* *Shalom* seems uneventful; a novel without a plot. It seems like nothing is happening. In the film "Witness," the barn-raising scene is a beautiful example of *shalom* in an Amish culture, but things only really get interesting when Harrison Ford starts using his fists. Further, peace can seem superficial; sometimes, so-called peacemakers withdraw from problems rather than facing them.
- *"Peace is too big."* It is for exceptional people who have special power or extraordinary skills. It is not for ordinary people like us.
- *"Peace is unrealistic."* It doesn't work. The attacks on the United States on September 11, 2001, demonstrated that the world is a violent place. Of course, many countries had known this long before 2001. Talk about peace seems idealistic. Peace is fine in theory, but it doesn't work in practice. What works—what really changes things—is violence. This may not be nice, but it is true to human experience. In light of this, talk of the church as a culture of peace is unreal. And we Christians are called to be real.

There is something valid in each of these statements. If we care about peace, we must do our best to listen deeply to the reasons why people find peace problematic. We may not agree fully with what they say, but they point to things that we must take seriously. For example, "Peace will dilute the gospel" seems incoherent if the gospel is actually, as many New Testament passages indicate, the "gospel of peace" (e.g., Acts

10:36; Ephesians 6:15). But the person objecting may be referring to certain Christians who have been more committed to peace than they have been to Jesus, or to reconciliation with the Muslims than to reconciliation with God. The objections thus invite us all to listen well and to think further.

Augustine said peace is unrealistic

To us, the objection requiring the greatest attention is the last one—"Peace is unrealistic." The world is violent. Cultures are corrupt. "9/11" has shown the world as it really is. Life as many people experience it, and as we read about it in the newspapers and see it on TV, is marked by the competitive and often violent interplay of selfish persons and groups. It is violence, or the threat of violence, that brings change and that preserves justice. To propose otherwise is hopeless idealism. To adjust to reality is pragmatic and truthful.

Violence works. This view, which theologian Walter Wink has called "the myth of redemptive violence," seems in keeping with reality; looked at that way, it is "common sense."[6] Responding to this seeming reality, bishop Augustine of Hippo, in the beginning of the fifth century, gave theological ratification to the church's departure from the peace-church tradition of its earlier centuries. Not once did Augustine comment on the verse that was so important to earlier Christians: "They shall beat their swords into ploughshares."[7] But several times, when preaching through the psalms, he commented on Psalm 46:9, "He makes wars cease to the ends of the earth." He observed:

This text has not yet been fulfilled. There are still wars. Peoples still fight against each other for dominance. There are wars between parties, wars between the Jews, the pagans, the Christians, the heretics. Some fight for the truth, the others for falsehood . . . Perhaps sometime this text will be fulfilled. Has it perhaps nevertheless been fulfilled? Yes, in some people it has been fulfilled. In the "wheat" it has been fulfilled. In the "tares" it has not yet been fulfilled![8]

Ever since Augustine, most Christians have believed deep down that peace is possible only in our hearts or after we die. But as to peace on earth—between people groups and within the church—that is impossible, and Christians must reluctantly learn to use violence as a lesser evil in the cause of justice. It is not surprising that after Augustine, the dominant Western Christian traditions have talked little about peace. It is also understandable that, since peace was thought to be unreachable, Augustine and Ambrose introduced the Christian "just war" tradition as a means of limiting violence.

Across the centuries there has been, of course, an alternative tradition. It is the tradition of St. Francis of Assisi, who traveled to the Middle East to talk to Islamic leaders; of the Quakers, who from their origins have believed that truth is stronger than power; of the Catholic Worker movement, who have demonstrated how justice and peace flow out of a determined commitment to do what Jesus taught. The Anabaptist groups (of which the Mennonites, referred to earlier, are one) quickly established peace as a central part of their identity. Menno Simons, for example, in 1537 saw peace as a sign of the true church:

> The regenerated people . . . are the children of peace who have beaten their swords into ploughshares and their spears into pruning hooks, and know war no more . . . Their sword is the sword of the Spirit, which they wield in a good conscience through the Holy Ghost.[9]

What all these groups in the alternative tradition have in common is significant. They believe that God has spoken definitively through Jesus; they sense that the early Church was on to something lifegiving; they mourn the fact that the churches of Western Christendom have lost their way and become conventional. Further, their eyes have been sharpened to perceive another dimension of reality, examples of which we encountered earlier in this chapter. This is the reality all around us, but which most people (including many Christians) tend to overlook: the tireless work of the God of peace who is making peace all the time, and who calls Jesus' disciples prayerfully to do what Jesus did—to see what God is doing and to join in (John 5:19).

Rediscovering the Gospel of Peace as Good News

Today, Christians once again are discovering that peace is central. They are discovering this for lots of reasons. They

are attracted to Jesus and to an alternative approach to conflict. They are discovering that Christians, in the name of
Christ, have committed horrendous atrocities from which
they wish to dissociate themselves. And they are realistic.
They are as aware as the so-called "realists" of the corrup-
tion, violence, death, and destruction in the world. But they
view it, not with hopeless, fatalistic resignation, but with
careful analysis leading to defiance.

War, they are convinced, doesn't work. Retaliation does-
n't lead to peace. Violence doesn't realize the purposes of
God. There are ways to deal with the injustices in the world
that are better than killing and coercion. Jesus is Lord! So he
offers to his disciples ways that are more creative than war
to deal with the challenge of Islamic fundamentalism, or any
other religious or ideological or national threat. For these
people, the church as a culture of peace is emerging in our
era as a real possibility.

These Christians are rediscovering familiar dimensions of
the gospel. They affirm that through Christ's cross and resurrection God has forgiven them and made peace with them.
And they are finding that, as a result, they have the privilege
of being part of a movement that forgives and makes peace
with others. They don't want to hoard the peace that God
gives them; they want to share it, pass it on, and let it transform the way they deal with enemies. This may at times lead
them to make statements about political issues, but that is
not the heart of their calling. Their primary task is to be "in

Christ" and, because they are in Christ, to learn how to become a people of peace who make peace. They know Jesus doesn't call his followers to be unreal. Jesus was in touch, and he knew that to take the hostility, the anger, the injustice, and the violence of the world seriously would take him to conflict and the cross. That's what he promises all who follow him. But they do not do this on their own. They put on "the whole armor of God," and equipped with that they join in the struggle "against the rulers, against the authorities . . . against the spiritual forces of evil in the heavenly places" (Ephesians 6:12-13). This approach to life is good news. It is our privilege to share it with others.

Through the conflict and the adventure of following the Prince of Peace, God is at work. As we shall see in later chapters, putting peace on our churches' agenda can bring a benefit to our churches—an authentic "peace dividend." It can transform our churches' "domestic" life together—our way of relating to each other and of making decisions. Furthermore, it can deeply affect our churches' outward life—our approaches to worship, work, war, and witness. In all of these areas, Christians are learning that the God of peace is working in many ways to make peace. As we experiment with these, we gain new insights and habits. We learn to say, "Our church is a culture of peace." And God smiles and gives us his benediction: "Blessed are the peacemakers, for you will be called the children of God."

4.
Peace Inside the Church

How do we describe churches that are cultures of peace?
Are they groups of people who say no to violence? Who have
a critical perspective on the wars their nations may wish to
fight? Might they have deeper questions?

Yes, we believe that they have deeper questions. As we
said in earlier chapters, a church that is a culture of peace is
rooted in the gospel which the church proclaims and attempts to live by—the "gospel of peace" (Ephesians 6:15).
This transforms life on every level, beginning with each individual Christian and extending to the congregation, whose
communal life transforms the individual's reflexes.

Dirk Willems

Like many children growing up in North American Mennonite families, I (Alan) often saw a seventeenth-century en-
graving. In this picture, a man, on the edge of cracking ice,
was reaching down to save the life of another man, who had
fallen through the ice into freezing water and was in danger

of drowning. As a child, I didn't understand much about the story. I knew it had taken place a long time ago in Holland—there was a windmill in the background—and I knew the name of the rescuer was Dirk Willems (See image at www.mbhistory.org/profiles/dirk.en.html).

But I didn't know what religious persecution was; I didn't know that the person whose life was being saved would be forced to arrest Dirk, leading to Dirk's execution for heresy. I didn't think about the unfairness of the situation, or about why God hadn't protected the life of one of his servants. I didn't ask whether Dirk did the right thing: should he have run away so he could survive, even if it meant his pursuer drowning? Above all, I didn't ask why Dirk did it. Why, instead of running away to safety while his pursuer drowned, did Dirk turn back to rescue his enemy?

Since then I have heard, and told, the story of Dirk many times. This picture has become a kind of Anabaptist icon. And the question of "why" has become ever more powerful in my mind. Why did Dirk turn back? It wasn't that he spent a lot of time thinking about what to do. People who drown in icy waters don't sink slowly; they go down fast. So when Dirk heard his pursuer's cry, he didn't have time to calculate outcomes or weigh ethical options. He had to react immediately. Dirk's response was reflexive. And so my question has become: what shaped Dirk's reflexes? How did he develop the reflexes and habits that enabled him to respond in an instant to his enemy's need?[1]

Developing the reflexes of peacemakers

Reflexes are important. We all, like Dirk, have reflexes—spontaneous responses when we are under pressure. Conventionally these are fight or flight. Either we attack what is threatening us or we run away from it. But Dirk responded differently, in a surprising and question-posing way. Dirk's reflexes had been trained by two things. One was his experience of Jesus Christ and his decision to follow him. As a faithful Christian disciple he had known God's love and forgiveness in Christ, and he had pondered Jesus' life and teachings. He knew that as a follower of Jesus he was called to love his enemies. Like other Anabaptists, he may have prayed that when under pressure he would do what Jesus had done and taught.

Also shaping Dirk's reflexes was the life of his Christian community. Reflexes like Dirk's are possible in individuals, but they are shaped in community—in a group of people among whom habits are formed and norms become normal. It is probable that Dirk responded as he did because he came from a particular kind of church, in which loving the enemy was an expression of loving the Lord, who had loved him to the very end, and who had taught Dirk to love his enemies.

There is twentieth-century evidence that reflexes like Dirk's can be learned by an entire community. In the 1930's, the parish of Reformed Christians of Le-Chambon-sur-

Lignon, high in France's Massif Central, received a most un-usual pastor—André Trocmé, who was a convinced Christ-ian pacifist. Week in and week out Pastor Trocmé taught his favorite Bible passages—the parable of the Good Samaritan and the Sermon on the Mount—to his people. So when the Nazis overran France and began to deport Jews to extermi-nation camps, the Reformed Christians of Le Chambon did something risky: they engaged in what they called "kitchen struggle." They took into their houses and farms a succes-sion of Jewish refugees, providing them with protection and cover until they could move on to safety in Switzerland. Eventually, at the risk of death and imprisonment, they saved the lives of over 3,000 Jews. Why did they do it? As one woman who kept a small hotel reported, her reflexes had been shaped by what she heard preached in church—the story of the Good Samaritan and the commandment to love her neighbor as herself: "I just could not have done anything else but help . . . the refugees."[2]

The formation of good character such as Dirk's, or that of the people of Le Chambon, did not depend simply upon their wanting to be loving persons. And so it is with us. Our good intentions must be embedded in Christian habits, in order for us to be transformed into good, Christ-like per-sons. Our lives must be "conditioned by habits to the right kind of likes and dislikes, just as land must be cultivated be-fore it is able to foster seed."[3]

Good habits and Christian virtues

A good habit drives our actions, and the habit itself is reinforced by repeating those good actions. A good habit shapes us to become a particular type of person, someone who is ready to act in certain ways. It's like gifted soccer players who have trained themselves in various skills needed to play soccer. They never think how they will kick the ball when it comes to them. They can act reflexively because they have developed good soccer habits.

Our habits shape us into a certain kind of people. As Christians we practice certain habits which enable us to act consistently according to the qualities of Christ. We become virtuous people, bearing the fruit of the Spirit (Galatians 5:22). Virtuous people develop "practical habits acquired by doing virtuous acts."[4]

In education, the most effective pedagogical method is to learn by doing. We learn to play the piano by playing the piano; we learn to swim by swimming. In a similar way, we learn to become loving persons by practicing love. We cultivate the habit of love. We develop the reflexes of love.

Does this mean that we can become peaceable individuals and virtuous communities by our own efforts alone? Certainly not. The Church, the body of Christ, is shaped by God's grace and the Spirit's power. Speaking of developing and practicing habits does not undermine God's grace. But God graciously uses habitual practices in the formation of

Christian character. God's habituating work reminds us that we should not turn divine grace into cheap grace. We are finite. We do not have the capacity to save ourselves. But as Christians, God calls us and enables us to act, to behave in certain ways.[5]

Let's think again about Dirk's life and death. Is the story too idealistic? Were Dirk's actions admirable in a "saint" but not applicable to us in the situations we face? Have we watched people who responded like Dirk did, or who responded with the more conventional reflexes of fight or flight? What were the results?

Thinking about Dirk's action, we believe, can help our churches become cultures of peace. For at the deepest level, the kind of church we are—whether a culture of peace or some other kind of church—is the product of our habits and reflexes. Our reflexes, like our values and our deep convictions, are shaped in community. They are shaped by the people with whom we share at the deepest level and with whom we have the deepest ties. We, like Dirk, are shaped by others.

Who shapes you? Who trains your reflexes? Your church? Your family and friends? Commercials, TV programs, and movies? If it is your church, does your church shape you to demonstrate, in your individual reflexes as well as in your common life, the teachings and way of Jesus to the world? Or are the people in our churches sometimes so bad at relating to each other that we don't have a chance of loving the enemy, because we don't love each other? Do we, in fact, sometimes treat each other like enemies?

The Church as a culture of peace

The Church is called to be a culture shaped by God whom we worship and by the story that we hear and tell. We Christians are not called to be against culture; our life and our witness will inevitably take cultural form.[6] But we have an exciting destiny—to become not a moral majority within our national culture, but a prophetic minority. For the most part in the West, Christians can no longer dominate (although the U.S. is perhaps a notable exception, where the neo-Christian right wields significant influence); in other parts of the world, generally, Christians never could do so.

Many of us now live in multicultural situations in which there is at least some solid respect for other cultural perspectives. So we now have the opportunity to develop a distinctive cultural identity growing out of our life in fellowship with Jesus Christ. We have the opportunity to develop Christ-like habits and virtues. These are distinctive practices that are in keeping with Jesus' teachings and way. Because we follow him and worship him, we give him the highest authority in our lives and the lives of our communities. Because we say, "Lord, Lord," we want to learn how to do what he says (Matthew 7:21). And as we do so, we embark on a journey of change, both individually and corporately.

Simply calling our churches cultures of peace will not necessarily make us a people of peace. It demands more than good intentions. Becoming people of peace requires a struggle between our God-given freedom and our human, finite limitations.

Created in God's image, we are endowed with a capacity for "self-transcendence," a "capacity for transformation," enabled by "glimpses of the eternal and the absolute in human nature."[7] This self-transcendence is our human freedom, by which we are able either to sin *or* to transcend the temporal and natural process in which we are involved.

But we are also finite beings. Having the capacity for self-transcendence does not mean the possession of perfection. However exalted our desire for self-transcendence, our finiteness is never obscured. Our self is always the finite self.

Because of our finiteness and sin, we have to make deliberate efforts to become people of peace. We cannot assume that our human nature will bring us onto the right path of becoming people of peace. We may have creative capacities to develop ourselves, but because we are also sinful humans, we need to be humble. All too often our human wants tend to bring us things which contradict peace. We need intentionally and with discipline to allow the Holy Spirit to shape our Christian character so that we can become like Christ (Romans 8:29; 12:2; Galatians 4:19; Philippians 2:5; 2 Corinthians 3:17-18).

Becoming a culture of peace requires us to bring into alignment both concrete behavior and thoughtful beliefs. We

cannot choose between them. The life of faith is life centered
in God and shaped by God according to divine grace, without putting away human efforts (Romans 3:21-24; 8; Galatians 5; I Corinthians 9:24-27).

Living as a culture of peace requires not just ideas and beliefs. It requires us to integrate our belief system, values,
commitment, orientation, lifestyle, and faith practices. Our
attitudes, behavior, and actions will shape and control our
entire way of life. As people of peace, we will have a consis-
tency between our internal awareness and our outward life.

In our corporate life as churches, we Christians have an
amazing opportunity. We can, in the words of theologian
Stanley Hauerwas, become "a manifestation of the peaceable
Kingdom in the world."[8] Or in the phrase of German
Catholic New Testament scholar Gerhard Lohfink, we can
become a "contrast society."[9] Those of us who are Mennonites can join fellow-Christians of other traditions in becoming "nonconformists," who are not conformed to other cultural options because we seek to be conformed to Jesus
Christ (Romans 12:2). We can develop new reflexes; we can
find that new things are possible or are worth working on.
It's this kind of church, worshipping this kind of Lord, that
enables the term "culture of peace" to make sense.

For the Church to make a contribution to the healing of
the world, we must allow God to change us, its members.
God longs to make us into the Body of Christ in whom Jesus
is alive, through transforming the conflicts we face in our re-

lationships and communities, through forgiveness, through prayer, and through the work of the Holy Spirit. God longs for us to be a people who believe that the Gospel is true, who become a people of peace and forgiveness. God invites us, in Christ, to accept his peace and to learn how to be peacemakers. Richard Chartres, Anglican Bishop of London, England, writes:

> At the top of the agenda of every human society is going to be the question of how we relate, how we live together peacefully, and the church as a school of relating . . . is very well-placed to make a contribution.[10]

We won't do this by avoiding conflict. We will do it by developing, as Dirk Willems and the people of Le Chambon did, habits and reflexes that enable us to deal with conflict positively and hopefully. Through Christ God has made peace with us. And God wants to equip us to make peace with each other—and through this to become peacemakers in the world. The church has nothing to offer to the world other than what it has learned to live in its own domestic life.

But how does this happen? How can we become a "school of relating"? How can we become apprentices who are learning the craft of peacemaking? How can we become a prophetic minority whose reflexes are enemy-loving and peacemaking? How can we become a culture of peace in a world of war?

The Disciplines of Peacemaking

The New Testament writers give us many pointers. And Jesus' teaching in Matthew 18 gives us a particularly important clue: we cannot make peace in the world until we have learned to make peace within the church.[11]

Verses 15 to 20 of Matthew 18 were a favorite passage of the sixteenth-century Anabaptists. These verses deal with a situation in which "another member of the church sins against you," and they establish a procedure for dealing with sin in the community. Experience suggests that where there is conflict in the church, there is at least a perception that members have sinned against each other. This passage offers principles that can apply generally to tensions in our church relationships.

Jesus assumes that there will be problems in the church. In Matthew 18, verse 15, Jesus gives instructions about what to do "if a brother/sister sins."[12] He does not indicate that this is surprising. People sin. Indeed, sins in relationships become evident when people take relationships seriously and share their lives on more than a superficial level. In the church, people sin; sometimes "they" sin against "us." Of course, we also sin against others—in Matthew 5:23 Jesus invites us to remember that our brother/sister may "have something against us"—and that we have a responsibility to take action to address the other's perception. In either case, it is clear that there will always be sin and conflicts in the church. The question is: how do we handle them?

Jesus says, "Go to your brother, go to your sister." Jesus' instruction is not to "keep the peace" but to enter into the conflict. Don't avoid the conflict, Jesus says. Face into it. Speak the truth, not *about* your neighbor but *to* your neighbor. Don't complain to someone else. Instead, go directly to your brother or sister. Jesus says, go directly to the person "when the two of you are alone." Don't gossip. Why? Because when we complain about somebody to a third party, and do not speak to them directly, we're treating them like an enemy. We're often seeking to build up an alliance of people who think like we do, against a brother or sister. It is very common for people in conflict to do this. We call it "triangling." It is especially unhelpful if the triangle is a way to avoid addressing the conflict and ends up perpetuating it and escalating it by inappropriately drawing in a third party.

An enemy is someone we talk *about* but not *to*. An enemy is someone we don't listen to. An enemy is someone whom we depersonalize and label. In Matthew 18 Jesus says: be direct; treat your apparently erring fellow-Christian as a brother or sister and not as an enemy. This requires directness, even confrontation—and confrontation of a particular kind.

Many cultures today are indirect cultures, in which it is difficult to talk directly to the brother or sister in conflict. However, most cultures have recognized ways of trying to address and resolve a conflict. So it is important to find creative ways to make contact and not to use our culture as an excuse for avoiding contact with the "other." Perhaps we have to talk with our fellow-believer in the presence of a third person whom both of us respect, such as an elder in our community or the village chief, whose function is to save everybody's face during the conversation. Or perhaps in our context there is another way to do this. The point here is that we need to find a culturally appropriate way to address the issue directly to and with the other member of our community when tension has arisen between us.[13]

Jesus-style confrontation is marked by clear, non-blaming speaking and active, deliberate listening. Jesus indicates that the initial objective of approaching the other person is to achieve a hearing. Four times (in verses 15, 16, and twice in verse 17 of Matthew 18) Jesus emphasizes that the other person is invited to listen. Jesus calls his disciples to engage in a process in which both participants give and receive perspectives. When this process begins, we don't know what will happen, because the process is a dialogue. By speaking, we may discover a new clarity in our view of the situation; as the other listens she may find a new understanding of herself—and may be challenged to repent. But we may also discover that the other person has a truth, or a perspective or a pain, that transforms our understanding. We may even discover that the sin is more on our side and the judgments we have made about the situation are faulty, and thus that we need to repent. For this kind of communication to happen, clear speaking and attentive listening are essential skills.

Jesus offers a process for dealing with unresolved conflict. If this one-on-one conversation doesn't lead to right relationships, the process continues. At every stage, Jesus emphasizes listening. We are to take one or two others along, in order to confirm what is said by listening well, with the initial objective that the other party will listen. The ultimate goal, of course, is that the other brother or sister will be regained and the community life restored. If the other person refuses, then we are to "tell it to the church." However we interpret this, the matter then becomes one for community discernment. But if the offender refuses to listen even to the church, what then?

Then such offending persons are to be to us "as Gentiles and tax collectors." Jesus is clear that listening is a core value of the community. By not listening, these persons show that they place themselves outside the community. They do not honor its core values; they will not allow their reflexes to be shaped by its reflexes. They have chosen to exclude themselves from the values, habits, and reflexes of the Christian community. They have made themselves outsiders. It is easy for the church to treat unrepentant brothers or sisters as outsiders. "Let them go. It's their choice."

Perhaps the Pharisees of Jesus' day would have said this, too. They were concerned primarily with proper observance and ritual behavior. But Jesus calls for a more difficult way. He says to treat the excluded brother or sister as a Gentile and tax collector. And how did Jesus himself treat Gentiles and tax collectors? With love and hope. The challenge is to recognize that the brother or sister who has refused to listen has distanced him/herself from the new culture of the messianic community. At the same time, the challenge is to draw the excluded brother or sister back into fellowship. There *is* a change in the relationship; the change in language in verse 17, which describes the other as the "offender," indicates this. But this is not abandonment. Even if the person can no longer be treated as a full member of the community, Jesus is calling his disciples—and is calling us—not to give up on the person, but to go the second mile, seeking to restore that individual to the life of the community.

Jesus promises to be present in this peacemaking process: "I am there among them" (verse 20). Often Christians have applied this verse to any meeting at which a few believers have gathered together. But from the context it is clear that Jesus promises to be present when his disciples are engaged with the challenges of community life, practicing the art of loving confrontation and trying to practice the skills of good speaking and good listening. So when we are about to speak directly to someone whom we have offended, or who has offended us, we can pray: "Jesus, you promised to be among us; please be with us now as we differ and as we seek your way."

This is teaching for forgiven sinners. It is not for a pure church, but for a church of people whom God has forgiven.

Immediately after this passage in Matthew's gospel, Jesus reminds Peter that the members of his community are to forgive without limit—70 times seven (18:21-22). The great American Baptist preacher and civil rights leader, Rev. Dr. Martin Luther King, Jr., caught Jesus' meaning when he said, "Forgiveness becomes an attitude, not an isolated act." Jesus then goes on to tell the parable of the "unmerciful servant" (verses 23-35). Jesus is telling his disciples: when you go into conflict, you go as forgiven people to other forgiven people—and your motivation to forgive will be your realization of the magnitude of the forgiveness each of you has received. We are all debtors; our peacemaking is rooted in grace! So we go to confront our brother or sister with humility—but we go, because truth in relationships is necessary in the church.

Jesus' teaching about conflict and peacemaking in the church is basic to being a culture of peace. It connects us to the heart of what we believe as Christians—about God's infinite love for us, about God's forgiveness of us in Christ, about God's call to us to be a people who forgive. And it gives us impetus to practice the confrontive art of peacemaking in order to make forgiveness practical.

Jesus does not promise that his teaching in Matthew 18:15-20 will always lead to "success." Sometimes a direct approach to someone who has offended us will lead to healing self-disclosures and a wonderful repair of relationships. At other times this may not happen. People may refuse to listen, or we ourselves may abort the process. There are situations in which a significant power imbalance can make a direct approach difficult or seemingly impossible. However, we note that Jesus has constructed a process ("Take one or two others along with you") which seems in part designed to deal with power imbalance.

Jesus was passionately concerned that his disciples not be deflected from intramural peacemaking. And it's striking: when Jesus equips his disciples with the disciplines of peacemaking, then he calls them "the Church" (*ekklesia*).[14] When Jesus talks about the Church, he says nothing about structure, governance, or style of worship. But he does talk about a community that is reconciling and reconciled. For Jesus, the Church is communities of his disciples who are being disciplined into communities of peace.

5.
Attitudes and Skills for Peace

Conflict is normal in life

"Thou shalt be nice. Always be nice. Yea, I say unto thee, niceness is the essence of being a Christian."[1] With his tongue in cheek, international peacebuilder John Paul Lederach has suggested that Christians often live by an unwritten rule in relation to conflict with one another: "Always be nice."

But on the question of conflict, Jesus was revolutionary. He never said, "Be nice." He didn't sweep conflict under the carpet. He clearly saw that conflict is normal. Jesus' own peacemaking activities led him into conflict: "I have not come to bring peace but division" (Luke 12:51). And his disciples after the resurrection also had conflict. The composition of their groups led to problems and conflict. It was bound to, for God was drawing together astonishingly different people—people who didn't belong together—to be members of communities of peace. And in any event, new religious movements such as the early church always have conflict. It seems to be a rule that where people are serious about life and issues, differences are inevitable. Conflict was present in the Christian movement from the outset. But the biblical accounts make it clear that this conflict was often important and useful.

Some cultures hold out the possibility that conflict can have positive outcomes. For example, the Chinese character that refers to conflict or crisis consists of two symbols, one of which means "danger" and the other "opportunity." Conflict can indeed become a danger that may destroy human relationships between the conflicting parties and cause loss of life and property. But conflict can also become an opportunity for the conflicting parties to transform their relationships and their social system in order to make the whole community healthy.

One example of this is Acts 6:1-7, the first recorded community-wide conflict in the early church. It was a conflict the Hebrews and the Hellenists. The church's system of feeding people daily was not working, and the weakest people in the community—the widows among the immigrants (Hellenists)—were being neglected. The Hellenists complained. This led to conflict, and a fascinating process ensued.

The leaders of the messianic community in Jerusalem didn't criticize the complainers; they took the complaints seriously as an indication that there was a problem. So they called the entire community together. They reminded the people of their holistic vision (feeding people as well as proclaiming the Word), and then they established an interactive decision-making process in which all the people were full participants.

The result was heartening. The entire community chose men from the weaker group (judging from their Hellenistic names) to help with the distribution, so that everyone was fed and the Word continued to be proclaimed.

Here is an indication, from the church's earliest days, that friction between differing groups can be productive. God's Spirit works, not just through prophetic words, but also through good process. God uses an interactive approach of discussion and truth-telling to clarify issues and to move communities forward. Conflict can be necessary to bring about God's good purposes. And as Carolyn Schrock-Shenk has observed, conflict can be the route by which we learn more about ourselves, the other person, as well as about God.[2]

But note the implicit warning: where conflict is not acknowledged, where people fear conflict or think it is wrong, the whole situation will get very unhealthy. The results will be thoroughly unpleasant: anger, depression, explosions, broken relationships, people damaged and alienated from the church. How often this has been the case! Christian churches have tried to avoid conflict; they have done everything they can to "keep the peace" as long as possible. But the result has been explosions of anger and hostility, leading to broken relationships and the splitting of churches and conferences. In many countries, this kind of behavior has made Christians a byword for bad conflict. Speaking personally, the Anabaptist-Mennonite tradition in which we stand has been no different. It may have emphasized peace, but its history has been characterized by many divisions.

Our societies have trouble with conflict

We Christians have trouble receiving Jesus' teaching and putting it into practice. It is hard for us. In most cases we live in environments, in our surrounding cultures, that are not conducive to good conflict or to peacemaking. In general, ours is a world of polarization, of adversarial thinking and acting, of winners and losers. And churches unfortunately tend to function much like the rest of society, or even worse than that society, rather than providing a hopeful counter-cultural witness.

Our churches can learn to handle conflict well

Regrettably, the culture of our churches is often notorious for its poor conflict. Non-Christians, insofar as they know of us, sometimes mock us because of our strife and hypocrisy. But it doesn't need to be like this. Our churches can become Christian cultures of peace which handle conflict well, as an aspect of our peacemaking.

The basic skills for handling conflict well are not difficult to understand, but it takes a lifetime to integrate them well—and so this is an ongoing challenge. Just as a good soccer team or a fine orchestra is not produced in a day, so also a culture of peace needs time to develop. Learning to be peacemakers will be a task for our churches until the end of time. As Christians who love peace, we are put to shame when we compare ourselves to soldiers who train themselves in rigorous disciplines to prepare for conflict. Just as soldiers train themselves in the skills of battle, so we, who want to be peacemakers, also need to train ourselves in the knowledge and skills necessary for peacemaking. To work at this, our churches need visionary leaders who model and teach Jesus' way of peacemaking to all church members.

We think of one such church—Oxford Road Church in Mexborough, England—where this has happened. In this church there had been severe conflict. But in recent years, there was extensive, practical teaching about how Jesus' Matthew 18 process could be put to work. For some time, on the wall of the church next to the praise banners, there were posters reminding the members of what is involved in peacemaking. One begins: "THE STEPS TO TAKE. One to one. Tell no one else. If this fails, take someone else . . . " This is not a perfect church. Perfect churches don't exist. It is, rather, a church which has been willing to learn to use Jesus' means of dealing with the inevitable imperfections and is finding unity in its life and witness.

The Mennonite churches in Indonesia require prospective pastors to be trained in peacebuilding and conflict transformation so that they can handle conflict with knowledge and skill, both in their churches and in society. As a multiplying effect, these pastors will later train their church members in the same knowledge and skills. These churches are building a peacemaking culture. Similarly, in their document "Agreeing and Disagreeing in Love," Mennonite churches in the U.S. and Canada have attempted to educate their leaders in peacebuilding and conflict transformation (see Appendix I).[3]

Most congregations do not need less conflict; they need more. Not more destructive conflict, of course, but rather a much greater capacity to deal openly and constructively with the inevitable differences in perspective and tensions in relationships. They need to recognize that the absence of apparent conflict is not the same thing as peace. The Bible reveals a God who hates false peace. The prophets regularly denounced places of worship that proclaimed *"shalom, shalom"* where there was no *shalom* (e.g., Jeremiah 6:14; Ezekiel 13:10). When Jesus went to church (the temple in Jerusalem) he disturbed the peace—he upset the tables and exposed the injustice—in the cause of true peace (Mark 11:15-18). God longs for the peace of right relationships, a peace that is rooted in justice and is an expression of truth.

Being changed into peacemakers

God is a peacemaker and calls us to join in his ministry of peacemaking. This is why Jesus said, "Blessed are the peacemakers" (Matthew 5:9). The peacemakers will be blessed because, as children of God, they will share in God's task and reflect God's character. Jesus' disciples—who listen to Jesus, watch him, follow him—are being transformed into his likeness; we are becoming "conformed to Christ" (Romans 8:29).

And as people who have been infinitely loved and forgiven, we do not need to fear rejection as we follow him into conflict. Jesus has shown us that peace does not come without conflict, and he has assured us of his presence. So we can cooperate as he works in our lives, making us holy as he reshapes us so that we pursue the "peaceful fruit of justice" (Hebrews 12:11). We can be transformed as God teaches us the attitudes and skills—that is, the virtues—that enable us to make peace by having good conflict.

A virtue always reflects a combination of excellence and power. For example, a knife has the excellence of sharpness, a watch has the excellence of accuracy, a person who forgives has the excellence of ability to forgive others, even an enemy. A person may possess an excellent ability to welcome or embrace someone across cultural lines. But it takes more than excellence. There must be power to fulfill the function needed.

As Christians we may develop skills for peacemaking—listening well, exercising patience—but those skills need to be empowered by the Holy Spirit. Christian peacemaking is more than mastering techniques. Peacemaking virtues are more than mere skills. Virtues are skills and attitudes that we learn, not simply techniques which someone teaches us. As our churches develop the virtues of peacemakers, we may become excellent tools in God's hands to bring about reconciliation and restoration. Let us consider the attitudes and skills of peacemakers.

Four attitudes of peacemakers

• *Vulnerability*

Conflict is a part of life, in the church and outside of it. Conflict indicates that people have real concerns, that they feel passionately about things, and that power issues are involved. Healthy relationships between human beings are always based on the willingness to make ourselves vulnerable and to take the risks that may come up in that relationship. When we begin a relationship with someone, we do not know what will happen. That is what it means to have an open relationship. We cannot predict accurately whether the relationship will bring happiness or pain. Even an intimate relationship between husband and wife is an open relationship full of risks. Every good relationship requires vulnerability and risk. The crucial question is not whether we can avoid conflict, but how we can solve and transform conflict when it comes, and whether we will take risks with each other when we do get hurt.[4]

• *Humility*

We should expect to hear something of value from those with whom we have conflict. They, like us, are sinners. But they, also like us, are loved and forgiven and equipped with insight and vision. God's truth is bigger than we have yet seen, and we cannot get the full measure of God's truth without others. We should not impose our point of view on others and force them to comply with us. Nor should we simply give up our point of view and submit ourselves to others. Both attitudes are destructive because we either oppress others (forcing), or we oppress ourselves (giving up). What we should do is collaborate with others in humility.

We should assertively state our point of view and interests so that others can see what issues, in our opinion, are centrally important. But at the same time, we should also attentively listen to others' points of view and interests in order to see what, in their opinion, are the issues at stake. Peacemaking cannot happen without constructive collaboration between the conflicting parties, who take seriously and humbly both the issue (the problem as we see it) and the relationship (the way that we are treating and interacting with each other). God calls us to the biblical virtue of forbearance (1 Corinthians 13:7); that is, the willingness to walk with those who disagree with us in the search for transformation. Even though we might not see any immediate concrete solution before us, yet we are willing to walk with our opponents and share the pain. We do not give up on them. This is a challenge that may be especially real for leaders.

• *Commitment to the safety of others*

We observe that people function best when they feel safe
in expressing their views without being attacked, made fun
of, or stereotyped. If someone adopts a position that we dis-
like, or makes us feel insecure, we will not get into name-
calling, whether we might want to call them "liberal," "fun-
damentalist," "dinosaur," or worse.[5] We will try not to
wound people even when they are our enemies, because we
believe that God's desire is to build friendship out of enmity.

An interesting example of this was the inter-faith reconciliation between Muslims and Christians in Central Sulawesi, Indonesia, which took place partly because the ma-
jority-group Muslims were willing to assure the safety of
Christians. On one occasion when there was a training ses-
sion in peacebuilding and conflict transformation, the Christians were afraid to attend, due to the systematic sweeping
of Christians off some streets in the city of Poso. The Muslim participants came forward to protect the Christians and
to give assurance of their safety. This kind of commitment to
the physical safety of others enabled the process of reconciliation to begin.

• *Hope*

God, we believe, is at work making peace, especially in situations of conflict. We also believe that God has a vision for
the church and the world that is bigger and more profound

than we can imagine. So we do not give in to despair. We do not surrender to cynicism. We do not hand the world over to the authority and methods of the Evil One. We do not revert to violence, thinking that all other ways to transform conflict into peace are useless.

Violence is a form of self-justification by which people try to give meaning to human life. People take into their own hands what is actually God's alone. Violence thus poses an assault upon God. After all, our mission as Christians is not primarily to bring solutions to the world's problems, but to bring hope for redemption. We believe that Jesus is Lord of all, and that his Lordship can express itself in surprising ways—and in the most unlikely of places. We believe that the Holy Spirit is at work, and that all kinds of creativity can break loose—if we pray trustingly and if we vulnerably open ourselves to the Spirit's work.

In the past, the Holy Spirit was able to change the hardened heart of a tyrant like Pharaoh. And the Holy Spirit is still working, even now. Before 1986, people in the Philippines never imagined that the regime of the dictator Ferdinand Marcos could come to an end without violence. Before 1989, people in the world never imagined that the Berlin Wall that had separated the Germans for decades could be destroyed without violence. Before the early 1990s, people in the world never imagined that Nelson Mandela and P.W. Botha would hold hands to symbolize the reconciliation between the whites and the blacks in South Africa. All these are signs that the God of peace is at work in the world. They encourage us to have hope.

Four Skills of Peacemakers

While the right attitudes are important, these will rarely be adequate in themselves. We also need to develop certain skills if we are to be effective peacemakers.

• *Truthful speech*

Peacemakers are called to learn to communicate truthfully but lovingly, passionately but humbly. This is more than a matter of words. Ephesians 4:15 urges its readers to "*aletheuein* in love." This is often translated to "speak the truth in love," but its meaning is broader. It means to "truth in love," to communicate truth with the total loving person, with all our body language, facial expressions, actions, and decisions, as well as our words. This was very important to Paul—he repeated the concern later in the chapter. Let us "put away falsehood, and speak the truth to our neighbors" (4:25). And both times the reason is significant: because it is through truthfulness that a group of people become a community, members of one another in the Body of Christ (4:16, 25).

Truthful communication will involve *encouraging* each other—affirming the gifts of action and being that we offer each other, and saying "thank you" for these.[6] It also will involve being *vulnerable* with each other, expressing our needs, worries, and longings. And it will involve being *confronta-*

tional when necessary, in order to address real or perceived hurts and offenses, so that these do not fester and become a root of bitterness (Hebrews 12:15). As we learn to "truth in love," we will grow up into Christlikeness. And our churches will become cultures of peace in which good communication is taught and modeled.

• *Attentive listening*

Peacemakers are called to listen well. People in conflict care passionately about things, and they want to be heard. So we will develop the skill of paying close attention to what the other is saying. We will want to make sure that we understand the other person, and that we enter into the thought and experience of the other. We will want to demonstrate our understanding—perhaps through summarizing what the other person has said as a way of checking whether we have understood the other person correctly. We will seek to discern the core meaning of what the other person is trying to communicate, and we will avoid getting hooked by the barbs or negative gloss the other may include, which will most often simply be an expression of the person's feelings of hurt. So we will try to grasp what exists in that individual's mind and heart.

We want to empathize with the other's thoughts and feelings. And as we listen, we will want to convey to the other person that we are listening—by our body language, by eye contact, by our reluctance to interrupt, or by other gestures that are appropriate in our culture to convey to the other person that we are listening seriously. We will try to monitor our own minds, so that we do not stop listening as we race forward to think how to answer the other's points; instead, we will trust the Holy Spirit to give us the words to carry the conversation forward.

In his book, *Exclusion and Embrace*, Croatian theologian Miroslav Volf, whose family and friends suffered in the Balkan wars, gives us a theological vision of how God's truth emerges.

> We enlarge our thinking by letting the voices and perspectives of others, especially those with whom we may be in conflict, resonate within ourselves, by allowing them to help us see them, as well as ourselves, from their perspective, and if needed, readjust our perspectives as we take into account their perspective.[7]

Volf argues that God's truth is one and God's perspective is pure, not least because God sees from the perspective of all his creatures, and God loves us all infinitely. Our perspectives, in contrast, are true but partial: they are real to us, but they are always incomplete. We cannot get at the larger truth—God's truth—except in truthful listening companionship with others. We need, Volf argues, "double vision"—vision from our side augmented by vision from their side.

The Center for the Study and Promotion of Peace of Duta Wacana Christian University in Indonesia has experimented with creating this "double vision" in its training for peace-building and reconciliation. The leaders of the exercise ask the two communities in conflict to exchange experiences with each other. Further, they ask each group to write a conflict scenario based on real experience in which they feel the other group has treated them unjustly or misunderstood them. Then the facilitators ask both groups to exchange the scenarios they have written. Finally, each group performs the other group's scenario in front of the whole group.

During the preparation for the performance, each group may ask the group who wrote the scenario to clarify anything they do not understand. Thus the Christians, for instance, will perform the scenario written by the Muslims, and the Muslims will perform the scenario written by the Christians. In a different twist in such an exercise, facilitators ask people to switch roles in a roleplay. So the local government officials, for instance, play the role of the traders in a traditional market who, in the real world, are often oppressed by the public officers. And in turn, the traders play the role of the government officials. They are then asked to roleplay negotiating a dispute that has happened between them.

Through such a simple exercise, people gain new awareness, new sensitivity, and even new respect for each other. They are now able to see reality from the other's point of view and to empathize with the other.

For example, in one of the training sessions on peace-building and reconciliation between the Christians and the

Muslims in Central Sulawesi, Indonesia, the Christians learned that the alcoholic drinks which many Christians in the area like to make, sell, and consume really pose not only a moral problem for the Muslims, but also a religious problem. They also became aware that many conflicts between the Muslims and the Christians in the area begin with the trouble that one or more drunk Christians create in the Muslim village.

The Muslims learned that when they checked ID cards in public buses, which many Muslims like to do in some big cities in Central Indonesia, the Christians experience it as hurtful, humiliating, and unjust. When Christians were dragged out of public buses and beaten up on the street, simply because their ID showed the "wrong" religion, they felt they were being treated like animals. In one of the training sessions, the Muslims learned that there is a big difference between Catholic and Pentecostal worship. This was astonishing to the Muslims, because within Indonesian Islam, all groups have identical rituals.

It is also possible to provide opportunities for people from two communities to live in each other's context, even if only for a short duration of time. The theology students at Duta Wacana Christian University in Indonesia regularly have the opportunity to live in the Islamic boarding school for some time, and the *santris* from the Islamic boarding school, in exchange, also live in the dormitory of the faculty of theology of Duta Wacana Christian University.

In 1995, a Youth Discovery Team, sponsored by Mennonite Central Committee and involving youth from North America, India, and Indonesia, had the chance to be exposed to and live in various non-Christian settlings in India and Indonesia. Such opportunities are useful. They provide space and time for people from different communities to build empathy toward each other. They enable people from both communities to see the others as subjects who have dignity, not as objects to be conquered and defeated.

So we must, if we care about truth, listen to others. We must listen to the experiences of others. Young people must tell us what it's like to be 17 today. Older people must tell us things they have never been free to share, such as their experiences during wartime or during their youth. People in conflict with us must tell us how they see things in light of what they have lived through. We can develop reflexes to listen to people who disagree with us. There will always be debates within the church, and there should be, because issues are rarely clearcut.

Many debates grow out of differences that are expressions of our humanity. Some of us are pioneers who explore new ideas and endeavors; others of us are settlers who conserve continuity. Some of us are extroverts, open, verbal, and energized by engaging with people. Others of us are introverts, nurtured by solitude and small groups. Some of us are gifted in mission, reaching out freely to others. Others of us are gifted in nurture, deepening lives and relationships.

Jesus got the balance right between these polarities. He drew perfectly on the old and the new, the outer and the inner, the reaching out and the deepening within. But we, as Christian communities, need to struggle to get the balance right, and to do so we need each other. God's truth, and God's way forward for us, will emerge as we listen well to others.

• *Alertness to community*

Peacemakers learn in community about the complex interweaving of human experience. Peacemakers are aware of the importance of differing generations. If the church is to be a school of relating, it is vital that there be elders who are taken seriously. Elders, according to theologian Gerald Schlabach,

> do not so much need to be old as to have lived the community's life well and deeply. Their word counts for more than others because it stands for much more than one person's opinion or self-interest.[8]

These are people, like Dirk Willems, whose reflexes have been sanctified by their friendship with the Prince of Peace. They have so much to teach simply by who they are. Their wise sayings and stories are also important. Churches that are cultures of peace must provide settings for elders to mentor youngers. Younger Christians, on the other hand, will have much to contribute to their elders—excitement, a lively memory of what it was like not to be a Christian, a willingness to question and test. It is through this intergenerational sharing that the wisdom, the skills, and the attitudes of peacemaking are taught.

Peacemaking is something that we learn by imitating role models who are masters of it. This is what lies behind the call of the apostle Paul to Christians to imitate Christ (Philippians 2:5-11; Romans 15:1-7), other Christians (2 Corinthians 8:1-15, 24), and even Paul himself (1 Corinthians 4:16; 11:1; Philippians 3:17).

Learning to be peacemakers is like learning to speak a language the natural way. We do not start by learning about rules and grammar, but we first listen to others who speak the language and imitate them. This is how we learn the necessary virtues of peacemaking. We learn through apprenticeship to masters who have learned God's story of peacemaking and lived it out. These masters are "the saints" who "present [us] with a wider array of ethical possibilities than [we] would have had if left to [our] own devices."[9]

Apprenticeship does not mean following exactly the paths that those saints have taken, as if their paths reflected the most correct stages of moral development. Rather, we use the models that these saints have demonstrated "on the highways, byways, detours, and straight and narrow paths that they have taken" to gain insights and wisdom for our own journey.[10] By looking at these specific saints, and not at general definitions, we discover what morally mature persons are like.[11]

Furthermore, peacemakers must remember that the *shalom* of a community will depend on its willingness to face economic questions. Justice and peace are interrelated. The absence of *shalom* in the Old Testament is signified by poverty, economic injustice, and political oppression. *Shalom*, on the other hand, is signified by the social harmony where there is no oppression in any form (Isaiah 54:13-14; Jeremiah 32:16-17).

The prophet Isaiah also speaks about a vision of "new heavens and a new earth" where "no more shall there be in it an infant that lives but a few days, or an old person who does not live out a lifetime." In the new heavens and the new earth, people "shall build houses and inhabit them; they shall plant vineyards and eat their fruit" (Isaiah 65:17, 20-21). That is why the prophets keep reminding the Israelites to work for peace wherever they are, even when they are in the enemy's land. Thus the prophet Jeremiah urges the Israelites to seek "the welfare (*shalom*) of the city [to which God has sent them as exiles] and pray to the Lord on its behalf" (Jeremiah 29:7).[12]

From New Testament passages such as Acts 6 and 1 Corinthians 11, church leaders have learned that it strains fellowship and distorts peace when some Christians are wealthy and others are economically struggling. Some churches sensitive to economic needs are committed to experimenting with radical measures to lessen inequality and to meet those in need. Where stark inequality exists, it is probable that relationships will be superficial and that un-just economics will undermine the peace of the church.

• *Community discernment and mutual accountability*

Peacemakers contend that a culture of peace is one which makes decisions in a way that is truthful, just, and corporate. We believe that the church meeting—a regular gathering for discernment and decision—can be central to the development of a peace church. Of course, church meetings are often scenes for point-making, power plays, and displays of argumentative power. But these distortions are the product of the church being too much like the world, of the church's failure to develop its own distinctive culture. It can be otherwise, when Christians learn together to realize "the unity of the Spirit in the bond of peace" (Ephesians 4:3) as they make decisions together.

The church must become the advocate of certain values and processes rather than of certain results. Leaders must believe that the Holy Spirit, who works among the people as well as the leaders, may produce something wiser than they could have anticipated. And when the people know that their views matter, they respond with a quality of enthusiasm and ownership that can be breathtaking.[13]

Why does the church have such strong moral authority? For two reasons. First, because its collective judgment reflects the judgment of the whole group and is more likely free of individual idiosyncrasy. Community discernment tak-

en by the gathered believers in church produces guidance for
individual Christians, as well as for communal witness to
the world. An individual Christian, apart from the believing
community, is powerless. Individuals need the moral discernment that takes place within the believing community.
The term *"ekklesia"* (the Church) originally referred to a
"parliament or town meeting, a gathering in which serious
business can be done in the name of the kingdom."[14]

> The church is God's people gathered as a unit, as a
> people, gathered to do business in his name, to find
> what it means here and now to put into practice this dif-
> ferent quality of life which is God's promise to them and
> to the world and their promise to God and service to the
> world.[15]

No one person is able to see all sides of reality at once.
Only God can do that. But our vision as Christians is en-
larged and clarified when we perceive reality together with
other believers. We can even enhance our vision further by
engaging in community discernment with people of other
faiths.

A second reason why the church has moral authority is
that it builds mutual accountability through thinking things
through together. Why is this important? As social beings,
we humans care about what others think. The scrutiny of
others is important and can encourage us to do the right
things. So, when we as church communities reason togeth-

er on a practical level, we can receive the evaluation and encouragement that builds healthy mutual accountability.

As members of the church, we are always under the moral evaluation of others. This is what it means to hold each other accountable. In the church we experience togetherness. But, more important, we learn to discipline "our wants and needs in congruence with a true story, which gives us the resources to lead truthful lives."[16] Our decision to join the church is essentially a declaration that we are willing to be held accountable by our fellow-believers in our Christian walk.

This is a primary reason why the early Anabaptists practiced believers baptism. The church, these Anabaptists believed, is made up of people who are willing to engage in the exercise of becoming each other's "keepers" (Genesis 4:9). The most crucial and important element in interpersonal relations is not our enjoyment of the presence of others, although this is indeed important, but our willingness to accept responsibility for each other.

On the journey: becoming a culture of peace

It's not completely clear what it will mean for a church to become a culture of peace. It will not be easy, and the changes required will be numerous. They will take time—because essentially we are looking at a process of cultural change within the church. And such a change of culture can only take place over the medium- to long-term, through a range of strategies sustained over time. We have already seen some of these necessary changes: new attitudes and reflexes that enable a constructive handling of differences; "truthing in love"; good listening; expecting God to bring insight through the other's experience; holding each other accountable; believing that the Holy Spirit is at work to bring about Jesus' way of peace on the earth—now.

All of this requires that a church who is becoming a culture of peace must undertake two fundamental tasks: empowering the individuals in the church, and empowering the structures of the church.

First of all, empowering individuals. How do we shape the character of individual Christians to become peacemakers? Through the educational and worship practices of the church. For example, we need to evaluate the materials we use in teaching baptismal candidates, in classes for new church members, and in children and adult Sunday schools. Do these teaching materials equip our people, both adults and children, to live the peaceful way of life? Do they impart the necessary knowledge and skills for peacemaking?

Peace education in the church and in Christian schools is also vital. We must train our pastors, our elders, deacons, and all church members with the knowledge and skills for nonviolent conflict transformation. We need to design curricula for peace education and to study biblical peace texts closely and expectantly in all areas of our church life—including in our worship. Have we made peace a central theme in our worship? Do we regularly preach the gospel of peace? Do we pray earnestly for peace? Does our church calendar include a Peace Month or a Peace Sunday?

Second, empowering the church's structures. Have we established a procedure in the church to address and transform in nonviolent ways the conflict that emerges inside and outside the church? Churches which do not have such procedures risk trying to hide the conflict or burying it. Hidden conflicts can grow and become like time bombs that can eventually destroy the whole congregation.

Many churches have committees, each one dealing with particular concerns or interests: youth, women, mission, worship. Perhaps the church should have a peace committee. It would be in charge of educating and training church members for peacemaking both inside and outside the church. It could serve both the church and the wider society through advocacy and mediation to transform conflict whenever needed.

There is no master plan for the transformation of our churches so that they can become cultures of peace. Each church will learn things in its own order, in its own time. But any church that sets out to transform itself to become a culture of peace will be on a journey. Gerard Hughes, a Scottish spiritual writer who has gone on many pilgrimages, has stated this wisely: "It is better to travel than to arrive."[17] Woe to the church that arrives! It will not be a culture of peace. But in greeting the Messiah, Zechariah was surely right. God's mercy was at work "to give light to those who sit in darkness and in the shadow of death, [and] to guide our feet into the way of peace" (Luke 1:79). And this way will transform not only reflexes of Christians and the domestic life of their churches, it will also transform their churches' witness and life in the world. We shall turn to this in our next chapter.

6.
Peace in Worship

"Grace and peace to you." What difference does it make to our churches, and to the world, when we take peace as seriously as grace? What difference does it make when we allow "the God of peace [to] sanctify us *wholly*," not just as individuals or in bits of our lives, but comprehensively—making us peaceful, holy, in all the dimensions of our life (1 Thessalonians 5:23)?

Earlier in this book we have contended that it makes a big difference when we allow peace to help shape our identity as churches. It changes the way we think and behave.

Furthermore, there is a "peace dividend" for our churches. This transforms our churches' culture; it helps build communities of people who are learning the skills and disciplines of peacemaking. As we want to demonstrate in this and the following chapters, this also changes our church's witness, our way of living in the world that God loves, and our way of serving it.

Living in a world of multidimensional conflict

In the 1980s, many people in the West were afraid of nuclear war in Europe. The world of the Cold War was a polarized world, divided between two power blocs, both of whom had nuclear arms. Since the Cold War, the world seems more complex than it did then. There is a new polarization and many Westerners are still afraid. In the post-Cold-War world, new conflicts have emerged. Suddenly many people are aware of intermingling cultures, tribes, ethnic, and religious groups.

Throughout the Cold War this multicultural world had been there, but it had been suppressed; now it has emerged, with cultural and religious identities that fragment nation-states and that ignore political borders. Now many people in the world are aware and proud that they are Muslims, Christians, Buddhists, or Hindus.

These clashing cultural and religious groupings—the Serbs and the Albanians, the Palestinians and the Israelis, the Kurds and the Turks, Muslims and Christians, Sunni and Shi'ite Muslims—have deep histories. And they can elicit immense passion and lethal violence. So the conflict is not out there. For many of us, these differences characterize and enrich our own neighborhoods. Ours is a multicultural world, and many of our neighborhoods are multicultural. This reality won't go away, which means living with complexity and conflict.

New polarizations emerge. Much of the world is preoccupied with the struggle between radical Muslims and the West. This exploded into the consciousness of Americans on September 11, 2001. Since the catastrophic hijackings of that day, the attention of the United States and, because of its power and actions, of much of the rest of the world, has been focused on a "war against terrorism." Scholars speak of a "clash of civilizations," with a sense of inevitable conflict and war between Islam and Christianity. In Indonesia, where the world's largest number of Muslims lives, more and more Muslim women wear *jilbab*, and Muslim men wear white robes, *sorban*, and grow long beards, sights that were not common some decades ago. Everywhere in Indonesian cities we can now find stickers, posters, and banners which say, "We are a Muslim family," or "I am proud to be Muslim." These signs do not simply demonstrate faithfulness to a religious command. They reflect a feeling of insecurity next to Western civilization. They send a message to the global community that Indonesian Muslims will hold their ground and keep their identity intact in the face of the sweeping force of Western civilization promoted by the United States and other Western cultures. In many parts of the world, Christians and Muslims are living as neighbors, at times happily, and at times with misunderstanding, tension, and even arson and killing.

Another polarization has been growing in recent decades which people in the West try not to think about. It is the growing divide between the North and the South, between rich countries that are becoming richer and poorer countries for whom a globalized economy has brought increasing poverty and misery. This polarization is not only outside the church; it is at the heart of the global body of Christ, and it is present in our own worldwide family of Anabaptist churches.

So this is the setting for our churches' life and witness. And this is our belief: as our churches discover how to be cultures of peace, they can have an impact for God and for good on our world. In this chapter we explore how this will deepen our worship; in later chapters we will look at how this will transform our approaches to areas of work, war, and witness.

Peacemaking worship

How, as our churches learn to be cultures of peace, will our worship be transformed so that we are more involved in the world? Isn't worship an intramural activity of the Christian family, mainly for members of the church? All too often worship services seem to have nothing to do with the world outside. Worship services at times are like the first astronauts, just back from the moon, isolated in quarantine. Nobody wanted the moon to contaminate the earth.

That's how it is with many churches and their worship; they quarantine themselves from the world. They don't want the world to contaminate what happens in the church. And they don't believe that their worship can make any difference to the world outside. This leads to unreality and to phony worship.

The worship of the church should be a truthful encounter with God, who loves the world, and who wants to empower his people to participate in his mission to the world. God is a personal God, and God is eager to meet with us as beloved children. But God is also Lord of history, and God is serious about being Lord of all peoples and nations, principalities and powers. Furthermore, worship is a meeting with other people in God's presence. Through this meeting with God and with each other, we see the world in a new light.

Worship "reconfigures the way we view our world, giving us 'new eyes to see.'"[1] And we change. Adoration transforms us; it gives us new reflexes and equips us to do God's work in difficult situations. And somehow, mysteriously, things change, too, on the earth and in the heavenly realm as the result of our worship. Worship is the motor of history; it is an engine for God's great project of peacemaking.

Identity: We acclaim Jesus as Lord. When we gather to worship God, we gather "in Jesus' name" to confess that "Jesus is Lord." This is powerful. All around us are lesser lords, lesser allegiances. We are citizens of countries, and that is important; we may have a job or profession (as a nurse or farmer or teacher or caregiver), and that also gives us a sense of identity.

But our primary identity is Christian. The early Christians, when the authorities cross-examined them, said simply, "I am a Christian."[2] They had a term for themselves— "resident aliens" (1 Peter 2:11), people who could be at home everywhere but who were fully at home nowhere. The earliest Christian creed was "Jesus is Lord!" That creed boldly contradicted the creed of the Roman empire—"Caesar is Lord." When we proclaim Jesus as Lord, we Christians in all times and places assert that our ultimate loyalty is to him.

Every day American children in public schools are required to pledge allegiance "to the flag of the United States and to the Republic for which it stands." Some Christian parents oppose this and instruct their children to stand quietly with their hands at their sides. Two American Mennonite theologians have recently proposed that American Christians should instead express primary loyalty "to a Trinitarian God known most fully in Jesus Christ."

> I pledge allegiance to Jesus Christ,
> And to God's kingdom for which he died—
> One Spirit-led people the world over, indivisible,
> With love and justice for all.[3]

Worshipping is pledging allegiance. When we worship God in Christ, when we say "Jesus is Lord," we pledge allegiance to him. If there is a conflict of sovereignties, it is Jesus whom we will obey. So his teaching is authoritative for us, and his way is normative.

It is by the Spirit that we make this confession of our allegiance and we make this confession in worship. It is in worship that we express our bond to the whole story of Jesus Christ and commit ourselves to what the confession is about—orienting our lives in adoration and obedience to the one who is our Lord.[4]

As we gather to proclaim Jesus as Lord, we open ourselves to seeing the world from his perspective. In worship, we use our Lord's words and tell his stories. By doing this we come to see reality in such a way that Jesus makes sense. And if Jesus makes sense, a lot of things that pass for common sense in our culture don't make sense. Jesus' teaching on wealth, peace, truth, enemies, sex, and trust is not good twenty-first-century common sense in any culture. The early Christians were often accused of being insane (Acts 26:24; *Acts of the Scillitan Martyrs* of 180, AD[5]). As we worship God, God gives us "liberation from common sense" and encourages us to "cultivate holy madness."[6]

So when a church that is becoming a culture of peace worships, it engages in discernment. As members, we seek the perspective of our Lord. What in our life and experience is in keeping with the way, truth, and life of Jesus, who shows us the Father (John 14:6-9)? What, in contrast, is worldly wisdom which God wants to unmask and discredit? Our worship will lead us to a yes and a no that will change the way we live. As we worship, God will give us eyes to see, leading us to choose God's way and to reject aspects of the seductive sensibleness of our age.

We affirm solidarity with God's global family. Because there is one Lord, ultimately there is one people who acknowledge his gracious rule. By grace we are adopted as children of the same King, and so we are brothers and sisters in an incredible family, made up of people from every tribe and nation, in which there is "one Lord, one faith, one baptism" (Ephesians 4:5). Wherever around the globe Christians gather, we acknowledge this fundamental fact—in Christ we are one in our praise and one in our belonging. The implications of this are prophetic. Our worship is a reminder to the world of "the arbitrariness of the divisions between people . . ."[7] To help us remember this reality, John Stoner, a Mennonite peace activist, revived a slogan first proposed in the 1950s (in a slightly different form) by M. R. Zigler, a Church of the Brethren leader:

> Let the Christians of the world agree that they will not kill each other.

Stoner suggested this to an ecumenical gathering and meant it to excite surprise. He did not mean that Christians should kill non-Christians; he is firmly committed to the gospel of peace and to loving all enemies. But he wanted to shock people into thinking about their inner identity.

We live in societies that program us to think of ourselves

and other people primarily according to race or nationality; we are Americans or we are Indians. Of course, in America today there are millions of Muslims, and in India there are millions of Christians—but that's not how most people think. Stoner seems to be saying to his fellow Christians: get your priorities right! Get your identity clear! We agree with Stoner.

We Christians are people who are one in Christ, who are brothers and sisters because of God's grace, who share bread and wine at his table, and whose ultimate human solidarity is with other Christians in all countries. When a national identity takes precedence over our Christian identity, terrible things happen. A devastating example is the nuclear bomb that in 1945 destroyed the Japanese city of Nagasaki. The bomb was dropped from a U.S. plane, piloted by Catholic crewmen who were given spiritual support by Catholic chaplains, onto a target whose epicenter was a Roman Catholic cathedral at the heart of the largest Christian community in Japan. The bomb wiped out two orders of Catholic nuns. War causes deep wounds everywhere, including within the body of Christ.

When churches become cultures of peace, their worship repudiates these perverted loyalties. To make the desecration of God's family more difficult, we who are members seek ways to remember the whole picture. We keep in touch with Christians around the world, exchanging letters, photos, and emails; when people from other countries visit our churches we listen to them expectantly. In many countries in the majority world, Christians are known and introduce themselves simply as "Christians"; not as "Baptists" or "Methodists" or "Mennonites." This is done to remind Christians and to give witness to society that all Christians belong to one body.

We remember God's story. The worship services in the Bible tell the story of God's actions more than they do anything else. From the Song of the Sea (Exodus 15) through the historical psalms (such as Psalm 78) and the Passover rituals (Exodus 12) to the worship of the New Testament churches at shared tables, the emphasis of worship is on remembering: "Do this in remembrance of me" (Luke 22:19). All of these acts of worship are means of remembering the story of God.

Why is this important? Because we humans are people whose identity is shaped primarily by the stories that we hear and tell. Our beliefs and our sense of selfhood are rooted in our experiences and in the stories that we have discovered to be true. Telling and re-telling the stories helps us know how to align our behavior with the character and purposes of God.

The community to which we belong determines a certain part of who we are and what we will become. We adopt the historical drama of our community, and we participate in its continuity. The community's perspectives, convictions, and ways of behaving determine our personal self-consciousness and our journey.[8] No actions, words, virtues, or even character can make sense apart from the story of which we are a part. We cannot answer the question, "What am I to do?" without first answering the prior question, "Of what story or stories do I find myself a part?"[9] "Finding oneself means . . . finding the story or narrative in terms of which one's life makes sense."[10]

The biblical writers knew this. They knew that the story of God and the people of God was strange. From the calling of childless Abram and Sarai to leave their securities in order to become the parents of multitudes through the breaking down of insider/outsider barriers through the work of Jesus Christ—this is a countercultural story. Its themes and values are odd. It contends that God prefers to work in an upside-down way among marginal people; it assumes that God is active. Christian worship is designed to etch that story deeply into our consciousness. So we hear and tell the story, ponder its depths and ambiguities, celebrate it—and by God's grace we continue it.

We live within many stories. Hearing, re-telling, pondering, celebrating, and continuing God's story is a challenging task. That is because we live within a multiplicity of stories—stories of our extended families, our professions, our nations. Some of these stories are inadequate, sick, or destructive. We cannot, however, simply deny these stories or force them into an artificial harmony. But we can choose God's story as the primary one which will shape our lives. When we become committed to God's story as revealed in the Bible, in Jesus Christ, and in the continuing life of God's people in the Holy Spirit, we find that it is sufficient to guide us to the values and virtues that will shape our Christian character. We can allow God's truthful story to form and train our character. It is the story that provides "the skills appropriate to the conflicting loyalties and roles we necessarily confront in our existence."[11]

The church plays an essential role as a hermeneutic community. In other words, it is a community that describes the world as it is, and that interprets the world in the light of the story of God as found in the Scripture. The church does this task of interpretation primarily in its worship. We learn to interpret one narrative (our own stories) through another narrative (the story of God).

Through its worship the church helps us to discover the "central metaphor," the "meta-narrative" through which we see reality and upon which we arrange, explain, analyze, and interpret moral precepts. That central metaphor shows us the true nature of God, of human existence, and of the world. What really counts in human life? According to Jesus it is love. At the center of his life and teaching Jesus imparted love—love for God, love for one's neighbor, and love for one's enemy.

This injunction to love is more than mere information about a Christian value. Jesus also demonstrated how love behaves. The heart of God's story is salvation history lived out in the world. This history culminated in the life, ministry, death, and resurrection of Jesus Christ. It is a divine story, which provides us basic convictions that are decisive, normative, and ultimate, for they help us to see reality "under the mode of the divine."[12]

In every era, Christians have faced the temptation to replace the story of God with other stories, stories that seem more sensible and that make powerful humans feel better about their wealth and violence. Some of these "sensible" stories are fundamental, underlying many others. Two such deep stories are "the myth of redemptive violence" and "the meta-narrative of military consumerism."[13] What do these mean in ordinary language? "The only thing that works is violence." "Might makes right." "I deserve to be better off than my parents were." "Well, the armaments industry provides lots of jobs." "We'll give the people in our church a choice; either they follow our leadership or they can go elsewhere."

We are constantly fed a diet of spin, which is designed to shape us according to the dominant stories of our society and to make us pliant, well-adjusted, inwardly-violent consumers. If we accept and live by this story, there's not a chance of our churches being cultures of peace.

That's why it's so important in our worship to tell, ponder, and celebrate the story of God. Think about it: do your worship services tell the story? Is the Bible read well, so that its story comes alive? Is there room for testimony, which recounts the story of God's actions in our own lives? Are there reports from the world church, which tie us into the bigger story? Are the sermons true to their primary task—passing on God's story from generation to generation? Do the words and rite of the communion service communicate the story? All of these can help us to remember and can inspire us to praise God—and also to live differently. If we tell God's story in our worship services, we'll be less likely to be choked by the world's violent spin.

We cry out to God for the world. The biblical writers urge us to intercede—for the peace of Jerusalem (Psalm 122:6), for kings and for all people (1 Timothy 2:1-2), and that God's Kingdom may come and God's will be done on earth (Matthew 6). We come to worship as people who know God's peace and whose churches are coming to be cultures of peace. So, as we gather, we hear the cries of the places where peace is denied. We listen to the cries and we join in them, praying to the God of peace who hears the groans of the inarticulate and receives the prayers of his people. God's Spirit helps us in our praying (Romans 8:26-27); and our prayers make a difference on earth (Revelation 8:3-4). We struggle with evil in our prayers—"against the rulers, the authorities, and the cosmic powers of this present darkness" (Ephesians 6:12). We contend with powers that diminish and impoverish people, and that express themselves in injustice, war, racism, scapegoating, and persecution.

The prayers of God's people can have astonishing effects. Twenty-five years ago, no one would have thought the following things to be possible—the fall of the Berlin Wall, the end of the Cold War, the end of apartheid in South Africa without massacre, the peace process in Ireland. But some churches, with persistence and passion, prayed for these things. "He makes wars cease to the end of the earth; he breaks the bow, and shatters the spear; he burns the shields with fire" (Psalm 46:9).

When we pray, we are entering into the work of God. We are praising God for all the places where his *shalom*-making is happening in new and exciting ways. We are interceding for human *shalom*-workers—including some of our own members whom we commission—whose power is minimal except through the power of God. And somehow, through our prayers and the prayers of many others, God can change the world. "History," wrote theologian Walter Wink, "belongs to the intercessors, who believe the future into being."[14]

What impossibilities are we interceding for at the moment? Right relations between Christians and Muslims? Between men and women? Between whites and blacks? Between the Tamils and the Singhalas? A worldwide abolition of nuclear weapons? The eradication of poverty and injustices? The protection of street children? The outreach of the church to the least, the last, and the lost?

Can the church be a culture of peace without intercession as an integral part of its worship? It's unthinkable!

We sing our theology. Our songs and hymns are important. We may talk theology, but we really believe what we sing. There is power and potential here for energizing and envisioning cultures of peace. But there is also danger. Some Christians are committed to inherited songs. They love the old hymns and defensively repudiate anything that seems emotive or new. The beloved hymns can at times be individualistic and pietistic.

Other Christians are committed to new songs. They reject old hymns and want to worship in ways that are relevant to contemporary cultures. But as they sing these new songs, Christians can be giving voice to the world's theology of power and domination. Outsiders might hear these new songs as threatening and offensive. In Indonesia, for example, a Muslim clergyman once said that Muslims hate Christians because Christians sing songs that are insensitive toward Muslims. For example, one Christian song says, "Our Lord will stamp on our enemies" (which are understood to include the Muslims); another song declares the intention of Christians "to win Indonesia for Jesus," which implies putting Christian-Muslim relationships within the framework of winning and losing.

Both of these approaches—singing the inherited songs and singing the new songs—are essential, but both can strait-jacket the discipleship of the church and offend other people. Churches that are becoming cultures of peace need to draw upon the artistic fruits of God's Creator Spirit, both across the centuries and in the present. They need to "bring out of their treasure what is new and what is old" (Matthew 13:52). They must draw upon those contemporary songwriters who, inspired by the vision of *shalom*, give poetic and musical expression to the theology and experience of a peace church. Cultures of peace will pray for the emergence of new songwriters in their midst. The songwriters' work is important. What we sing is what we internalize; it will be with us when we're weakest, when we're old, and when we're dying. Let's choose wisely what we sing, because we believe and become what we sing.

God reconciles us and forgives us, so we will pass on reconciliation and forgiveness. When we worship God, God is the main actor. God is at work pursuing the Kingdom goals of "righteousness and peace and joy in the Holy Spirit" (Romans 14:17). God is at work reconciling us to himself, healing us of our sicknesses of body and spirit, forgiving our sins, restoring our inner motives and our priorities. Worship is one of the main tools in God's workshop. It is God's gift, which God uses to refashion us in the divine image and to end our alienation. This is gracious and glorious, a source of endless wonder and thanksgiving.

The worship of cultures of peace will not stop when the worship services are dismissed. It will continue throughout the week. In the Bible, God's command to his people is not simply to accept his forgiveness; it is to act forgivingly to other people. It is not simply to be reconciled to God; it is to be reconciled to other people. Paul put this economically: "Welcome one another . . . just as Christ has welcomed you" (Romans 15:7).

Miroslav Volf has noted that Paul's injunction "is to make
the pattern of divine action toward us a pattern for our actions toward the other."[15] According to this vision, every
church which experiences and celebrates the reconciling
and forgiving love of God is called to be a culture of peace.
It is called to receive and celebrate the reconciliation that
God offers us, and then to pass it on to others and not to
hoard it.

Some of these other people, by God's grace, may join us
in the reconciled community. This is why the early Christians developed the rite of "the kiss of peace."[16] It was a
means, within their worship, of celebrating the peace of
God, and where there were broken relationships of restoring them, so that the church, as a reconciled body, could offer reconciliation to others.[17] Jesus told his disciples that
making peace between brothers who are at odds with each
other is more important than the offering (Matthew 5:23ff)!

Jesus went further by reminding his disciples that they
should offer forgiveness to others because it is the precondition for God's forgiveness of them. "Forgive us our debts,
as we also have forgiven our debtors" (Matthew 6:12). Jesus pursued this even further: "For if you forgive others
their trespasses, your heavenly Father will also forgive you;
but if you do not forgive others, neither will your Father forgive your trespasses" (Matthew 6:14-15).

By emphasizing the importance of forgiveness, Jesus turned the Old Testament pattern upside down. In the Old Tes-

tament, reconciliation had to be worked out first before forgiveness could be granted. So the high priest came before God to bring the offerings on behalf of the sinner, in order that the sinner could once again be reconciled with God. But Jesus insisted that for genuine reconciliation to take place, forgiveness has to be offered first. Jesus embraced the sinners and tax collectors while they were still sinners, in order for them to be reconciled with him and restored into community. Jesus even died for us on the cross while we were still sinners (Romans 5:8). So forgiveness is the precondition, not the product, of reconciliation.

A church that is becoming a culture of peace will always ask: in our worship do we allow God to reconcile us to himself and to each other? Does our worship empower us to be God's ambassadors of *shalom*-making and reconciliation in the world? A culture of peace will find ways to create rituals of forgiveness and reconciliation in the church, so that those who have sinned against others may hear God's gracious voice of forgiveness, "You are forgiven; do not sin again."

Even though forgiveness and reconciliation should be worked out directly between the victim and the offender, it is important for the offender explicitly to hear God's promise of forgiveness. Through the rituals of forgiveness offenders can hear and realize that the loving God has accepted and embraced them.

God feeds us at the communion table,
making us a people of equality, nonviolence,
and reconciliation

Communion is an immensely rich ceremony, a rite with many layers of meaning for peacemaking Christians. This richness is not surprising. The most characteristic place for Jesus to be with his disciples was at the table. In our time, it is also at the table that we meet with Christ, who breaks the bread and pours out the wine and reveals his presence to us. There are many communion themes—covenant, boundaries, discipleship, economic justice, mission—which are important.[18] But we will concentrate our attention on three other themes—equality, nonviolence, and reconciliation—which are central to the worshipping life of cultures of peace.

- *Equality.* At this table we all are equal. All of us have sinned and fallen short of the glory of God. And all of us are offered the same quantity of Christ's limitless food and drink. Communion is thus an expression of the radical egalitarianism of the gospel.

- *Nonviolence.* The communion table is also an expression of the gospel's nonviolence. Jesus said to his disciples, "Remember me. Remember my sacrifice for you. Remember my way of dealing with my enemies. Remember my teaching. Receive my presence and my grace. Pass these things on to others." Communion offers us a rite by which we remember that Jesus has made things new. Jesus was the last scapegoat. After him there is no need for further violence.[19]

- *Reconciliation.* Christians treasure communion as a place to experience God's forgiveness, received through Jesus' sacrificial death and resurrection. But communion is also an occasion to remember how we have offended another, to admit that we have sinned against another, and to recognize the need for reconciliation. Many times in communion we are aware only of God's justification and forgiveness of ourselves. It is easy to forget that communion challenges us and calls us to respond in acts of reconciliation.

God offers us forgiveness both individually and corporately. But God's forgiveness is not cheap. The gospel of Christ requires us to commit ourselves to genuine reconciliation. It calls us to pay attention to those we have sinned against. We cannot simply go quietly to the communion table and ask God to forgive us and assume that everything will be okay.

God offers us forgiveness, yes. But first God goes to the oppressed, to the victim, and makes solidarity with her. This is what Jesus, himself the innocent victim of violence and injustice, did on the cross. He cried out, *"Eli, Eli, lama sabachthani?"*; that is, "My God, my God, why have you forsaken me?" (Matthew 27:46). Jesus here identified with other innocent victims. This is also why he prayed, "Father, forgive them; for they do not know what they are doing" (Luke 23:34).

Jesus' cry and prayer on the cross do not represent the cry and prayer of a sinner, but the cry and prayer of one who is in solidarity with the victims. Who are victims? They are, for example, little girls who have been sexually abused by their own fathers, street children who are forced to work for money so that their bosses can buy drinks or drugs, housemaids who have to work for 20 hours a day without a decent wage.

In Matthew 5:23-24 Jesus reminds us that if someone has something against us (that is, if we have sinned against someone), we must seek reconciliation with them before we come to worship. Things must be made right between us and the ones we have offended. This applies to us individually as well as corporately, and it affects the way that the church observes communion.

The divine forgiveness that we celebrate in communion is available to us only when we go to those whom we have sinned against and reconcile ourselves; that is, we ask them for forgiveness. Jesus is not only present with us, the sinners. He is also primarily present with those whom we have sinned against. We will find Jesus before and amidst the victims of our sin. So when we take the bread and wine in communion, we are actually reminded of those people whose bodies are broken and whose blood is shed because of our sin. It is to them that we should come in humility and ask for forgiveness.

Churches that are becoming cultures of peace will find in the communion meal many ways to keep us filled with, and in tune with, our peacemaking Lord.

God shapes our vision and mission. Churches that are becoming cultures of peace experience a life-cycle of worship and mission.[20] To begin with, when we gather for worship, we bring "reports from the front." We bring the experiences and hurts and longings from our involvements in God's Kingdom work in the world. We reflect the violence and injustice, and we are agonized by the hardness and broken relationships.

Then, as we worship together, we encounter "the God of peace, who brought back from the dead our Lord Jesus Christ" (Hebrews 13:20). We tell the story of God and celebrate it. We learn the ways of God and come to view these as the path to abundant living. We praise God, give thanks, and make intercessions.

Worship thus functions as a filter; it purifies us, clarifying our vision. And it empowers us. It restores our belief and re-inspires us with God's grace and vision for the world. As we conclude our worship we realize that worship equips us for mission.

Re-visioned by our encounter with the God of peace, we go back into the world equipped with hope, vision, and spiritual energy. We will be in the struggle with principalities and powers. But we will find God at work, calling people to faith, suggesting new ways forward in intractable situations, and building cultures of peace in the wider society.

We will not go unscathed, but the God of peace will be with us. The tasks will be too large. We will fail. So we will come back to the worshipping church, bringing our brokenness and new stories of God's grace. And the cycle will continue. This cycle of worship is essential for a culture of peace: it heals us, energizes us, and keeps us on course. It links God's love with our lives and with God's world in a swirl of new creation. Worship is not quarantine: it is the heart and soul of a culture of peace involved with God's world.

7.
Peace in
the Workplace

People of new habits

It is possible for our churches to be cultures of peace! Although Christians have often been wary of peace, peace is at the heart of what our churches are meant to be about. We Christians are passionately committed to grace; we know that God has saved us not because of our achievements or goodness but because of God's infinite love and mercy. This excites us with wonder and praise.

If we wish to have biblical priorities we will be likewise passionately committed to peace. The New Testament writers habitually began their letters by coupling the two together: "grace and peace" (Romans 1:7, 1 Corinthians 1:3, and so on). What happens when our churches, like those of the New Testament, rediscover this coupling? It changes our theology and way of thinking. It deepens and enriches our churches' common life, our life together. Rediscovering

peace transforms the way our churches relate to others, and
our worship takes on a new reality and depth. In this chapter we will see that the God of peace can transform our work,
filling our life in the world with new creativity and peacemaking potential.

At work, shaped by the life of a peace church, we will have
new skills to offer, new attitudes, and new habits. The habits
are especially important. Theologian Stanley Hauerwas has
commented, "What we must do is help the world find the
habits of peace whose absence so often makes violence seem
the only alternative. Peacemaking as a virtue is an act of imagination built on long habits of the resolution of differences."[1]

What difference do the habits shaped in a peace church
make in our daily life and work? Recently a Christian mother had the following experience. Katie and her two little boys
were baking cookies—chocolate chip cookies. The aroma
filled the kitchen as the first trays of the goodies came out of
the oven. The cookies cooled on a large tray, tempting the little boys as they hung over the table.

Katie glanced out the window. At this time in the after-
noon, high school students were walking home past the
house. Katie noticed with alarm that a lot of these young
people were gathering in a swirling crowd on the sidewalk
just out in front. Someone shouted, "A fight! A fight!" Others pushed in to see what was happening.

A natural impulse would have been for Katie to gather up
the little boys and peer out at the violent scene from behind

the kitchen curtain. But Katie's reflex impelled her to do something else. She grabbed the tray of warm, fragrant chocolate chip cookies and ran out into the crowd calling, "Anyone want a cookie? A chocolate chip cookie?" Hands reached eagerly for the cookies. The crowd dispersed.

In a culture of peace, habits change. Most of us—those of us unemployed or at home with children, as well as those in paid employment—have the opportunity to work and to invest our creativity, skills, and sweat for the good of others. When our churches become cultures of peace, we discover that we have new things—and new habits—to offer.

We will see the world differently. Who we are and what we do are closely connected to the way we see reality. We make decisions and choices within the world we see. And what we see indicates what we most care about in our lives.

In order to *do* rightly, we need to *see* rightly. Human beings "differ not just because they select different objects or facts from the common world, but because they see different worlds."[2] This is the explanation behind the different acts in the story of the good Samaritan (Luke 10:29-37). The good Samaritan saw the half-dead person with compassion and helped him, whereas the priest and the Levite, perhaps fearing personal pollution, passed him by. In this story, we can see that people performed different acts not because they saw different facts, but because they saw the same facts with different eyes.

A moral way of seeing reality comes from learning to see the world more truthfully. Morality, in a fundamental way, has to do with the "total vision of life."[3]

What we see actually depends not on what lies in front of our eyes, but on what is in our hearts and minds. This is why the church plays an important role. The church can help us to discover and to see the conditions around us through the eyes of faith. This is difficult because our vision is often clouded with distortions and illusions. The church can help us see more deeply, past surface appearances.[4] We must not expect this to be a simple task. Ambiguities will remain. But these ambiguities can be seen from a special perspective.[5] James McClendon puts this well:

> To be sure, the world is not Christian; there is fallenness and rebellion and ruin enough here. But the eyes through which we Christians see the world are redeemed eyes; it is exactly through these eyes that we must be trained to look . . . [6]

We will do things differently. As we noted in chapter 4, in a culture of peace, Christians learn to follow Jesus' procedures, outlined in Matthew 18:15ff, to practice "truthing in love," and to see with "double vision."[7] So a distinctive kind of Christian is formed. These Christians are people who are humble because they know they are forgiven sinners. They are committed to good speech and good listening and good process. They are good observers, who believe that it is important to see through the eyes of others as well as their own.

They are not afraid of conflict because they believe that God can use conflict to bring peace. They are full of hope because they believe that God is at work in every situation to move history towards the reconciliation of all things in Christ (Colossians 1:20). These habits, convictions, attitudes, and skills are immensely useful in the world. They enable things to happen better.

In any church, there are Christians who already are peacemakers in their work situations. They often don't recognize this, but the realization may come to them as a surprising, gracious gift from God. An information technology consultant recently wrote about his discovery: "[I have realized that] by facilitating dialogue, or acting as a go-between, I was in fact mediating peace and encouraging relationships to develop. God is not only interested in my work, but even in acrimonious business meetings, God wants to work through me to establish the values of his Kingdom there." This man is a *shalom*-maker who now recognizes that he is a *shalom*-maker.

Christians in cultures of peace believe that God is at work in the children's nursery as well as in the corporate boardroom. We believe that God is alive and in the business of peacemaking. God, we believe, can change things.

How do we know that changes we see are the work of God? How can we evaluate the results of our own peacemaking efforts? We need to realize that our confession of Jesus Christ as Lord is more than just an individual or sectarian ideal. It is a claim about all of reality. The whole world and all aspects of human culture are under the lordship of Christ. There is no necessary contradiction between Christ and culture, or between creation and redemption. So, even though we may have a positive view toward the world, we need clear ways to distinguish the work of God from the work of the evil one. We need to discern peacemaking from evil-making.

In the life, death, and resurrection of Jesus Christ we find the criteria we need to make these distinctions. Churches that are cultures of peace are the discerning communities in which we discover together God's will for us and the world. It is in and through these churches that we discern God's work in the world and reflect on whether or not a particular historical event reveals the way of Christ.[8]

Not everything that happens, even in relation to our peacemaking efforts, is divine and is from God. To be sure, God enters our world. We confess the incarnation of Christ, and this always means that God has entered the world to show what we can bind and what we have to loose (Matthew 18:18). But we must do all this with humility and prayer.

We will bring peacemaking imagination to our jobs. In churches that are becoming cultures of peace, Christians get new ideas; new possibilities spring to their minds. They are less likely than most people to sit back and be conventional.

So a peacemaking imagination can transform our work, altering the boundaries of the possible and inspiring us to try precarious new things. It's important for churches to tell stories of how this has happened.

Some stories are well-known, such as the founding of the Victim Offender Reconciliation Program (VORP) and other restorative justice procedures, which grew out of the hunch of two Christian Canadian probation officers that biblical justice involves a restoration of relationships. VORP-like programs have spread throughout North America and Western Europe, and have led to major changes in judicial practice.[9]

Other stories have to do with art, such as that of the peace-church sculptors who not long ago created a massive swords-to-ploughshares sculpture for Judiciary Square, Washington, D.C., made of over 3000 decommissioned handguns. This sculpture now stands as a witness to God's peacemaking. As one of the sculptors wrote, "Being created in God's image, I can also creatively strive to recreate a fallen world."[10] Something similar happened in the Philippines. An artist in Dumaguete created paintings on peace themes and recently conducted a peace arts exhibition, together with some other artists who share her vision of promoting peace in the Philippines.

Or the stories can have to do with music. On the island of Bali in Indonesia, a peace activist composed an interreligious peace song with the words, "Pray for the peace of humanity . . . *Shalom, Salam, Shanti, Siancay, Sadhu, Damai* . . . Humanity shall live in peace." The song has been translated into several local languages and promoted by the Center for the Study and Promotion of Peace of Duta Wacana Christian University. The song is proving useful in Indonesian elementary schools as a means of encouraging children to imagine a world in which people from different religions live together peacefully.

A pastor in Indonesia, who works part-time in a Christian radio station, saw an opportunity to do something risky. Through the local Association of Radio Broadcasting, he decided to approach the commander of a radical Muslim group, Hisbullah Shabillilah (the Soldiers of God), in the city where both the pastor and the commander live. When the pastor first visited the headquarters of the Islamic group, he saw that on the walls were lots of swords and banners, with "No Compromise!" written in big letters. But the pastor took time to befriend the commander of the soldiers and his followers and to have dialogue with them about peacemaking.

On one of his visits he noticed that something symbolic had happened: the swords and banners had been taken off the walls. And the Muslim commander promised to send his members to attend the training on peacebuilding and conflict transformation that the pastor was organizing.

In response to the December 26, 2004, tsunami disaster, the commander was eager to work together with the pastor and the Center for the Study and Promotion of Peace in a relief and trauma healing project in Aceh and North Sumatra.

One day the commander told the pastor, "If only I had known you four years ago, I would not have had to lose 50 of my children who died in Ambon and Poso [in a war between Christians and Muslims]. I used to think that spilling the blood of the Gentiles and the Chinese was *halal* (or permissible), but why is it different now? Is there something strange within me since I have learned to know you?"

Some peacemaking stories, such as that of the Empowering for Reconciliation with Justice Project (ERJ) in South Africa, are massive in scope. In the early 1990s, the ERJ trained over a thousand people with the skills of mediation and peacemaking, so necessary in a society in the throes of rapid change.[11] Others, such as the quiet efforts of Christians in the Parades Commission in Northern Ireland, are immensely important but quite unsung. Nobody involved in these initiatives would say that carrying a peacemaking vision into the workplace makes things easy. But it brings hope and new possibilities.

Peacemaking with other Christians and with people of other faiths

Some years ago a pastor in the Indonesian city of Solo established an interreligious and intergroup Peace Forum. The forum has worked intensively in various parts of the city to train and establish groups of mediators, consisting of people from different religious backgrounds.

Why was this necessary? For the past three centuries in Solo there has been a tendency for local tensions to escalate

into city-wide conflicts. The vision of the Peace Forum is to
have an interreligious group of mediators (about 20 mediators from five religions) in each village within the city to
handle local community conflicts as soon as possible before
they escalate.

In Makasar, Indonesia, the leader of 400 Jihad soldiers decided to disband his group after he attended the training sessions on peacebuilding and conflict transformation given by
the Center for the Study and Promotion of Peace of Duta
Wacana Christian University. A dialogue with Christians and
moderate Muslims in the training had changed his view on
how to solve societal conflicts.

Peacemaking in the workplace

Our peace convictions are tested in the real world. As we
have emphasized previously, we need to be critical of our
surroundings, including our places of work. Theologian Max
Stackhouse helps us in this matter by pointing out that we
need to be critical of the social-economic institutions around
us and discern what kind of spirituality underlies those institutions, including our own workplaces. Stackhouse suggests that we uncover that spirituality by looking at five aspects: vocation, moral law, liberation, sin, and covenant.[12]

Vocation. Every socio-economic institution, profit or non-
profit alike, owned and operated by Christians or not, has its
own specific vocation to minister to people in God's econo-

my. Each institution is to make its contribution to its society's well-being through its particular skills, services, or the products that it offers, even while it gains profit. Hospitals are for healing and caring for the sick; schools are for the search for wisdom and truth; business corporations are to promote the economic prosperity of society.

Since every institution has its own vocation, it should be proactive, not merely reactive, as it works for the well-being of society. Institutions should give attention and care to the victims of their bad policies, or of political and economic policies in society.

People whose values are shaped by cultures of peace will look at their workplaces and ask questions: What is the vocation of this workplace? Is it congruent with God's will for peace on earth? If it is, has it been faithful to its vocation? Has it fostered the *shalom* of society as well as of its shareholders?

• *Moral Law.* In a postmodern world, many individuals and social-economic institutions are reluctant to speak about moral law. They may be afraid of being accused of self-righteousness. However, the reluctance to speak about basic principles of right and wrong has caused many socio-economic institutions to become either legalistic or pragmatic—anything is okay as long as it is strategic and efficient. This has to do not only with the institution's internal policies but also with its outward policies.

Members of churches that are becoming cultures of peace will look at their workplaces and ask questions: Are the firms advocating moral values? If so, how? Through what channels? Are there signs of courage to debate whether policies and actions are right or wrong? Or are policies simply accepted on grounds that are legalistic or pragmatic?

• *Liberation.* A socio-economic institution can become liberating, but it can also become oppressive and excluding. In its planning and implementation, each institution should consider what kind of liberation it is going to bring about within itself and in society.

Members of churches that are becoming cultures of peace will look at their workplaces and ask questions. Is their workplace becoming a place of liberation, or of oppression and exclusion? Is liberation a fundamental consideration in the organization's planning and implementation? Does it treat its workers well and gain their support by respect and proper reward, or does it coerce their responses through methods of disrespect and oppression?

• *Sin.* The drive to foster production has often involved the destruction of world resources that God has given to humanity in creation. We humans have forgotten the Sabbath law that provides space and time for all creatures, human and non-human alike, to take rest and to recover. The distribution of goods often involves the sacrifice of some creatures. Some people gain disproportionately at the expense of other people. And through increased consumption, waste has multiplied.

Furthermore, socio-economic activities are often dominated by the oppression of others. Socio-economic institutions can become shrines to the worship of mammon; such false worship demands the sacrifice on its altars of human beings and other creatures. There is only one name for this: sin.

People who have had their habits formed by a culture of peace will look at their individual workplaces and ask questions. What sins has the firm committed in its production, distribution, and consumption activities, for which it should repent? Does the firm show any intention of balancing its activities with a provision for Sabbath? Does it distribute social goods (position, salary, reward, recognition, social ministry, and so on) without sacrificing others? Do its consumption activities reflect care for the durability, preservation, and sustainability of the environment? Does it seek to expand its operations through healthy competition, or through immoral means such as hostile take-overs, public deception, and the like? Does it respect its competitors as legitimate competitors, or as enemies to be conquered and annihilated?

* *Covenant.* Relationships among people in socio-economic institutions should be based on covenant, not power. These institutions should become places where power is

shared, not accumulated; places where there is pluralism of authority, not destructive centralization or homogenization; places where there is shared decision-making, not autocratic domination by an elite group; and places where all stakeholders participate appropriately in determining the course of the institution.

People whose sensitivities are shaped within cultures of peace will look at their workplaces and ask questions. Is the relationship between workers and managers respectful and dignifying, or is it authoritarian? Does the organizational structure reflect a just use of power, or the misuse of power? Does it implement and practice a structure of mutual accountability or a "frog structure," in which people are encouraged to lick up, kick down, and push aside?

By now it should be clear that it is helpful for churches, in the process of becoming cultures of peace, to provide training for their members in mediation and conflict transformation. We will be in positions to help our colleagues solve or transform conflicts in our workplaces. Colleagues can themselves learn the skills of peacemaking. The more people who are trained in these skills, the more wholesome the workplace will be.

We should persuade the leadership in our workplaces to offer training in mediation and conflict transformation for both managers and lower-ranking employees. Because conflict in the workplace can significantly reduce productivity, such training benefits the workplace as a whole. The use of power and violence to solve conflict in the workplace damages its entire environment. Unresolved conflict often leads to a decline in productivity. So it is less expensive for a firm to invest in mediation and conflict transformation training than to spend money and time on a repressive settlement of conflict.

Peacemaking in the home

If we belong to a family devoted to peace, our household will be run in a peacemaking way. One of the crucial issues is the way we raise our children.

Thomas Gordon suggests that we differentiate between discipline as a noun and discipline as a verb.[13] Most people agree that discipline as a noun is a good thing for our children. We want our children to have discipline. But people differ in understanding the necessity and meaning of discipline as a verb.

Many people think that in order for children to have discipline, they need to be disciplined or controlled. Good discipline, the noun, can never be achieved through *control*. Good discipline can best be achieved through *influence*.

Control evokes rebellion, resistance, retaliation, or lies. Sometimes children may comply with their parents' orders, but this compliance may be based on the fear of punishment. The psychological truth is this: "You acquire more influence with young people when you give up using your power to

control them. The more you use power to try to control people, the less real influence you'll have on their lives." Some of
Gordon's suggestions about noncontrolling methods are
worth mentioning here.

- *Finding the children's needs.* When children do things that
  we cannot accept, they always have some reason for their
  behavior. It is important for us to find what the children
  really need and to address it. This will require careful listening and sympathetic evaluation.

- *Using confrontive I-messages.* Instead of blaming children,
  we would communicate more effectively if we used an I-
  message to tell them what we are experiencing in response to their unacceptable behavior. For example,
  telling the children that we feel bad because they are
  treating us as mere drivers when they do not thank us for
  picking them up from school is better than reprimanding
  them with words of accusation.

- *Using preventive I-messages.* Different from a confrontive I-
  message, the preventive I-message lets children know the
  kind of behavior that we expect from them in the future.
  For example, telling them that we expect them to ask our
  permission first if they want to return home late, so we
  won't worry, is an example of a preventive I-message.

- *Shifting gears to reduce resistance.* Even when we use I-messages, children may respond with resistance. In such a sit-

uation, it is better for us to shift gears from an assertive posture to a listening and understanding posture. It is important for us to let our children know that we do not want to get what we need at their expense.

- *Problem-solving.* Sometimes these approaches (I-messages or shifting gears) do not work in persuading children to change their unacceptable behavior. If children persist, we need to work together with them in mutual problem-solving, which involves: a) identifying the needs, hopes, fears, and passions of each (parents and children); b) generating possible solutions; and c) evaluating and choosing a solution that both we and the children can agree upon.

- *Finding the primary feeling.* Parents often do not realize that behind their anger toward their children may be some deeper, more primary feelings. Anger is a secondary feeling. It can be another form of a You-message, and so it is judgmental and destructive.

If we are angry because of our children's poor grades, our primary feeling may really be that we are embarrassed by their poor performances. We get angry with them, but our primary feeling is that we are embarrassed. Our anger is a secondary feeling, a mask that is covering our embarrassment. It is important for us to pause for a moment whenever we get angry with our children, in order to discover the primary feeling that is making us angry.

God can change our location and our vocation

There are times when we become restless in our jobs. Sometimes, as a result of the Bible's *shalom* vision that is taught in our churches, we realize that we are no longer satisfied in jobs that are too easy; we are not really making a difference for God's kingdom. We may be open to a new job where our efforts address the pain of the world more directly. Our church may send a cluster of its members to live and work in a troubled urban area; we may move away from a position of security to a place on the front lines of shalom-making; or we may volunteer, as newly retired people, for an assignment which crosses borders and serves needy people. In any of these cases, we will be opening ourselves to the first of "the three R's" of evangelical prophet and community-developer John Perkins: "relocation, reconciliation, and redistribution."[14] Relocation—the gospel of peace can put us in a new place.

The gospel of peace can also change our vocation. The habits, attitudes, and skills that we are learning in the peace church may make trouble in the workplace. Our bosses or colleagues at work may reject the peacemaking imagination that we attempt to bring to our jobs. And there are times when we realize, with surprising clarity, that our jobs are incompatible with our worship of the God of Peace. For any of these reasons, members of churches that are becoming cultures of peace may find themselves in need of support as they leave their jobs and retool themselves for new vocations.[15]

David Cockburn is an English engineer who, after many years in a military electronics firm, left his job to do an M.A. in Peace Studies to prepare for work that he really believes in. Dave is a Christian on a journey. He was moved by visiting the Nazi concentration camp at Dachau; he cared deeply about the Yugoslav crisis and felt unable to do anything about it; he heard God inviting him to a new vision of his life through Isaiah 58:6-10; and he saw peace-church Christians doing new things in the area of conflict resolution, especially in Northern Ireland, that gave him hope. He wrote:

> It is through seeing them working in the area of mediation and conflict and bringing about real changes, by good understanding and an awareness of how to cooperate with God in these situations, that I have begun to see possibilities for change in impossible situations. This has led me on to try to understand more and to beware of acting without the understanding.[16]

Dave is a loss to the electronics industry, but he is now working at something that as a Christian he really believes in—becoming a volunteer mediator with Christian Peacemaker Teams in Palestine. He is an example of what happens when the God of Peace works in our lives. God changes us; God may also change our jobs.

8.
The Culture of Peace in Wartime:
Making a Difference Without Being in Control

The world is in turmoil. The newspapers, and sometimes the cities where we live, are full of violence and threat. People are angry and fearful. How can we be a people of peace in this kind of world? It's hard; we may feel odd to speak in favor of peace. And we feel insignificant; at times we may be afraid to speak out. It seems so futile! Why go to the trouble of trying to be a culture of peace when it's obvious that most people disagree, and when people can get rude, and even menacing, to those who don't fit in? Do we want to stand out?

Wouldn't it be smarter to keep quiet, or even to change the way we think? After all, so many Christians disagree with us.

What makes us so sure we're right? Why should our churches try to be cultures of peace? Why not urge our countries to
pursue "peace through strength" (to use the U.S. motto)? The
world is big, and we are small. We have no power, no control.
We are insignificant. Can we make a difference?

We believe that churches who are becoming cultures of
peace can make a difference. We will mention six ways. We
mention these humbly. We and our churches don't understand things perfectly. Further, we don't always live up to
our convictions; we are compromised in many ways. But we
believe that God's people, even if marginal and seemingly insignificant, can make a difference and are making a difference in a world that we cannot control. How can we do this?

By being ourselves. God calls us, as disciples of the Prince of
Peace, to be ourselves! Jesus says we are blessed when we
make peace (Matthew 5:9). So, in our families, schools and
jobs, let's "pursue what makes for peace" (Romans 14:19).
Let's make peace in our families, our schools, and our jobs.
Let's be creative, imaginative, surprising. Just as Jesus' resurrection surprised everybody then, so the church of the res-
urrected Christ should bring surprise to the world. In our
time, many people can only see deadends. Violence seems
to be the only way forward. But it doesn't have to be like
this. Christians, in the power of the resurrection, can work
creatively to bring about surprising alternatives. Resurrection today can mean that God's power of peace and life has

overcome and is overcoming the power of violence and death.

At work:

- We can do new things: as elementary schoolteachers we can pioneer a new program involving our students as mediators of disputes within the class.[1]

- We can do things that others aren't doing. At a time when most foreigners are leaving Israel, missionaries from a peace church are living in Nazareth, bringing Nazareth Village to life which will interpret to all visitors—Jewish, Muslim, and Christian—the way of Jesus. At a time when most Westerners are terrified of Iran as a country of radical Islam, a young Christian North American couple are a Christian presence in Qom, the center of Shi'ite Islam, studying Islamic theology. At a time when most people in Bihar, India, are afraid of the Maoist Communist Centre, a group of local Christians has renounced violence and kept in touch with the Maoists, who have treated them with surprising graciousness because "we are *very loving* to all and we sincerely try to do good to them."[2]

- We can do things in a different manner. At a time when people are severely polarized, we can witness about the contested life issues of abortion, capital punishment, and war with gentleness, pointing out the "seamless garment" of commitment to life that ties them together.[3]

As congregations:

- We can make a peace witness: a congregation in Landisville, Pennsylvania, bought 300 copies of John Roth's book *Choosing against War: A Christian View*.[4] Adults and teenagers gave it to friends; members intentionally left it in restaurants with a note to whoever found it: "Read this and pass it on." A young person even sent a copy to the U.S. Secretary of State.

Whatever our situation:

- We can simply find ways of saying: we don't think that war is the answer, for anyone.

What is the effect of these efforts? Who can say? But we affirm that we are sowing the seeds of peace. We have to remember that we do peacemaking, not because it works, but because it is faithful to Jesus Christ. The success of the church and Christians should not be measured by our effectiveness in society, but by our faithfulness to the gospel of peace. We do peacemaking, not because it can bring good things in the world, though it does, but because it is good in itself. We are simply called to do the things that are normal for Christ's friends and disciples. We are called to be ourselves, people of Christ's peace.

By warning. Christians from cultures of peace, even though we have very little worldly power, have a biblical perspective which gives us the power to see. And so we can lovingly warn others.

The world's power may be weaker than it appears to be. Things may not be what they seem to be. Military forces look immensely strong: Saddam Hussein was said to have weapons of mass destruction (and didn't have them); we know that America and France and India, among other nations, have weapons of mass destruction. These weapons are said to make nations strong. Christians from cultures of peace doubt these claims to strength.

Throughout the Bible, prophets like Isaiah spoke against people who trusted in military power—in "chariots because they are many, and in horsemen because they are very strong" (Isaiah 31:1). Isaiah had a different perspective: "When the Lord stretches out his hand [they will stumble and fall], and they will all perish together" (verse 3).

Jesus had this sense of the illusory quality of military strength. He looked over Jerusalem and wept over it: "If you, even you, had only recognized on this day the things that make for peace!" (Luke 19:41ff). Jesus grieved because the people, instead of accepting him and his way, were trusting in wea-pons. Jesus warned that disaster would come to people who trust in weapons: "Indeed, the days will come upon you, when your enemies will . . . crush you to the ground, you and your children within you, and they will not leave within you one stone upon another; because you did not recognize the time of your visitation from God" (Luke 19:43-44). This, says Jesus, is what happens to people who have faith in war.

So what, in wartime, do Christians from cultures of peace say? Like the prophets and like Jesus they warn, lovingly and compassionately. When advocates of war claim that violence will lead to a quick, neat outcome, peace-church people, like Jesus, remind them that they are seduced by illusion. Historical events are marked by irony; things don't turn out as people anticipate. Human endeavors have unintended consequences.

So the witness to government by people in churches that are cultures of peace will not be to give precise recommendations of policy. But we will tell the government, by our letters and by appropriate political action: "We're praying for you, and we're praying that you won't trust in chariots and horsemen; we're praying that you won't trust in smart bombs and cruise missiles. These weapons won't work. It's not that they won't explode or hit their targets (some of the time). Rather, the weapons won't bring peace. They will magnify hatred. And they will bring immense sorrow to the country that uses them, as well as the country that absorbs their use. They will bring immense grief to the world. So trust in God and turn around. Use your minds and imaginations to find ways to make peace with your enemies."

By expecting surprises. For Christians, being weak is no problem. That's the kind of people that God chooses to work with. Look at Jesus. Throughout his life he had little power. But he made the powerful feel very uncomfortable. And when the rulers put him on the cross, Jesus had no power at all; his strength was ebbing away, for he was dying. But in dying with almighty meekness he changed the world—for good. After the cross and the resurrection, things will never again be the same. Now we say: Caesar (the crucifier) is not lord, but Jesus (the crucified) is Lord. The victim becomes the victor. And the victorious victim changes the way we think about power.

That's the way it is throughout history. The most significant happenings are often weak and obscure. Luke 3:1-2 gives us a list of important people:

> In the fifteenth year of the reign of Emperor Tiberius, when Pontius Pilate was governor of Judea, and Herod was ruler of Galilee, and his brother Philip ruler of the region of Ituraea and Trachonitis, and Lysanias ruler of Abilene, during the high priesthood of Annas and Caiaphas, the word of God came to John son of Zechariah in the wilderness.

Who is important? What is significant? A conventional view will say it's the emperor or kings or governors or high priests. The gospel-writer Luke does not despise these; he gives a clause to each of them. But to John the Baptist, the hairy man in the desert, Luke gives a whole chapter! The early Christians, who were marginal and persecuted, knew that prophets are more significant than political leaders. They knew that throughout history, what's really significant is often taking place on the margins.

Today, Christians in cultures of peace know that we may be a minority, but we are a significant minority. We live in obedience to God and in sheer defiance of false confidence in weapons. Thereby, we serve the rest of the world that rejects us. We remind the rest of the world that there is another way, a way of love, of service, of humility, of wisdom. We learn to treat each other with loving, humble wisdom; we also learn to treat our enemies like this.

God gives us new ideas. Inspired by God, we experiment with new ways of thinking, acting, and solving problems. And what does God say? "Not by might, nor by power, but by my Spirit, says the Lord of hosts" (Zechariah 4:6).

By being a conscience to God's people. Christians from cultures of peace can be a conscience to the other parts of Christ's church. We can bear witness to the rest of the Christian church. Peace-church Christians (Anabaptists, Mennonites, Church of the Brethren, Quakers) are not the whole church. We are not right about everything. We have much to learn. But God has preserved us through persecution.

The survival of the Anabaptists of the sixteenth century was miraculous—most of the governmental authorities and churches tried to extinguish the movement and kill its leaders, but it survived. Why did it survive? Because God has given the peace-church tradition things to contribute; God has given it a part to sing in the Christian choir. Our part is similar to that of the Early Church, the church of the early centuries. It didn't have much power, but in significant ways we bear testimony to a similar vision.

In recent years, Mennonites have made a small impact. We have produced writers with some global influence: among them are John Howard Yoder, Ron Sider, and Fernando Enns.[5] This does not mean that we are in control; we are marginal. But we have begun to influence some other Christians.

In England today, Anabaptism (an historical and theological movement from which Mennonites stem) is attracting Christians of various traditions to join together in an Anabaptist Network. Many Christians are drawn to an evangelical tradition that sees peace at the heart of the gospel, that does not force people to choose between evangelism and peacemaking. Leading English Christians are calling themselves "Anabaptist-Baptists," "Anabaptist-Anglicans."[6] In Central America today, some Christians are calling themselves "Pentecostal-Anabaptists."[7] These hyphenated Anabaptists are a sign of the growing influence of the peace churches in a time of war.

By thinking about war in peacetime. In most churches, members during peacetime banish the thought of war. Indeed, they don't begin thinking about war until the bullets begin to fly. That is a difficult time to think clearly. When people are fearful and angry, when flags are flying, when the world is being polarized into people who are "on our side" or against us, between people who are "good" and those who are "evil," it is hard to discern God's will and word. In such a setting, it is extremely difficult to be creative, or to take a position most people will view as strange and unpatriotic. And it is extremely easy to be swept along with the majority.

If our churches are to be cultures of peace, we have got to think about war before emotions are high and the troops are about to roll into battle. We've got to think about war in peacetime. We who are privileged to be disciples of Jesus— we who have been moved and motivated by what the Bible calls the "gospel of peace"—have got to think about issues of war and peace before bombs are dropped or shots are fired.

Why do we need to think about war in peacetime? In part, for our own sakes, so we can be faithful disciples of the one who said "Follow me." Also, in part for the sake of other Christians, so we can be a resource for the wider Christian movement.

Christians in cultures of peace are not awkward cranks and oddballs; we are custodians of the earliest Christian vision which it is our privilege to share with all believers. We need to listen to the perspectives of other believers, who will teach us much about all kinds of important matters. But we also have something to offer which points other Christians towards the time when they will join in regaining the common, original vision of Christ's church.

So let's teach about war and violence. Let's especially teach young people in junior high and high school. How do

Christians settle differences? How do we cope with the contention and aggravation that we encounter daily at school and work? Through roleplays as well as through Bible study, we can help our young people think about the violence in their lives—and then apply the gospel of peace to their situations, as well as to other areas of life, including war. That's what we have been attempting to do in this book: to show that the gospel of peace applies not just to war but to our congregational life, our worship, work, and witness.

But, as we all know, our approach to violence and problem-solving is not the only one. So we should teach our young people the alternatives, which many people hold and which also are worthy of our careful and respectful thought. Broadly speaking, Christians across the centuries have had four approaches to war and violence:[8]

1. Christian Nonviolence/Pacifism: the approach, which underlies this book, is that of the Mennonites and other peace churches.

2. The Just War: the official approach of most Christian bodies.

3. The Crusade/Holy War: the approach that some Christians have adopted in "Crusades," which claims that God is on our side and that Christians may use any means against enemies who are evil.

4. The "Blank Check"/Realism: the approach that says that the government has more knowledge than we have, and

that we must do what the government says, even if it means using weapons or attacking targets in ways that seem wrong to us.[9]

It is vital that we explain all of these approaches. In studying war in peacetime, we will explore the last two of these approaches, while rejecting them firmly. We will reject the Crusade because it has diabolically adopted the cross in causes of falsely righteous violence. And it has left in its wake a hostility to the gospel of Jesus Christ that is well deserved and immensely hard to overcome. We will reject the "Blank Check" because it is idolatrous; it simply confesses that "Caesar is Lord."

On the other hand, it is indispensable that we, in churches that are becoming cultures of peace, teach approaches 1 and 2. We must teach the first of these, Christian Nonviolence/Pacifism, in every generation. This is the position that expresses our understanding of the gospel and helps give us our identity. By teaching it, we have the opportunity to make a distinctive contribution to the world. This much is sure: pacifism/nonviolence receives no encouragement from the world—from the media, from politicians, or from the boys in the locker room. Jesus' way of enemy-loving and peacemaking is odd, but we believe it's the way to life. It's how the Christians thought for the first 300 years before the conversion of the emperor Constantine.[10] It's our calling and joy to be true to that vision.

But it is also important for the peace church to teach our young people about the second approach—the Just War. Why? Because Just War is what most Christians say they believe in. When you ask people what their position is on war, many will respond, "the Just War." But if we take them seriously and ask them, "And what is the Just War?" a lot of them don't know. It is important that we understand Just War, so we can converse well with other people.

In churches that are cultures of peace, we can teach our people the broad history of the Just War. We can point out that the theory originated about 350 years after Jesus, as Christians attempted to win the adherence of the aristocratic elite of the Roman empire. Gradually this theory was adopted as the position of the Catholic Church and, after the Reformation, of the dominant Protestant churches.[11]

The sixteenth-century Anabaptists objected to this approach. While we in the Anabaptist tradition also reject Just War, we can converse with those who believe in it. We can understand that the originators of the Just War did not see it as a means of justifying war; rather, they saw the Just War as a means of deciding under what circumstances Christians can justly depart from the norm for all Christians, which is peace. So the Just War doctrine is a means of evaluating war. And it maintains that Christians may justify going to war only if war meets certain conditions; if it does not meet these conditions, the war is unjust and participation in it is sinful.

We provide criteria for a Just War in Appendix II. Briefly they state that a war will be just only if:

- there is a *just cause* (declared by a legitimate authority, in response to a clear violation of justice, with a right intention, with a probability of success, as a last resort);

- it is fought by *just means* (with discrimination [no intentional killing of noncombatants], wreaking damage that is proportionate—the war may not cause greater damage than the damage of the original wrong).[12]

These are, of course, matters of judgment, and Christians have often differed about how to assess these. The Just War theory has had good effects. It has led to international laws governing the conduct of war, and, in recent years, it has caused soldiers to be more circumspect about killing civilians than they used to be.

The Just War criteria have also led non-pacifist Christians to evaluate current wars, such as the Vietnam War or the American invasion of Iraq, as unjust wars. These Christians are "selective conscientious objectors."[13]

Other Christians, who might be willing to use violence in certain circumstances, are appalled that Christians would be willing to deploy and use weapons of mass destruction such as nuclear weapons. These Christians are "nuclear pacifists."[14]

So Christian pacifists and scrupulous adherents of the Just War theory can often work together. And, in any event,

Just-War talk is so common among Christians that believers of all persuasions need to be able to talk about the Just War theory intelligently.[15] Christians from cultures of peace will never have all the answers about war and violence. But we can make a difference by doing what many Christians tend not to do—teaching and thinking about war in peacetime.

Furthermore, Christians from cultures of peace need to do more than oppose war. They must work actively for peace. Baptist ethicist Glen Stassen has pointed out that when Christians discuss war, they often debate whether it is ever right for followers of Christ, in a just cause, to resort to violence. Some Christians argue that believers should never take life, whatever the situation. Others argue that Christians may reluctantly have to resort to violence, provided that it is carefully guided. Both sides assume that wars will take place and that the most important decision facing Christians is whether or not they personally can take part in the violence. This is an important debate for Christians.

But the real question is bigger than that, Stassen contends. How are we going to work with God to make peace? What alternative practices will we develop, what new approaches can we experiment with, to discover new ways forward in our violent world? Stassen, who is part of a group of cooperating theologians from both peace churches and churches who espouse Just War, invites us to engage in what he calls "Just Peacemaking." This consists of 10 practices which all Christians—whether or not they ever are willing to use violence—can use in making peace instead of war. Some of these practices are: (a) Using cooperative conflict resolution; (b) Taking independent, transforming initiatives to make peace, and to talk and negotiate with whomever we perceive as enemies; (c) Advancing democracy, human rights, and religious liberty; (d) Fostering just and sustainable economic development; (e) Supporting nonviolent direct action; (f) Acknowledging responsibility for conflict and injustice and seeking repentance and forgiveness.

Stassen does not suggest that these practices can abolish war. But he points out that in recent history the practices have, in fact, abolished certain wars, and that they "are incrementally changing the way nations relate." These practices do not end the debate about war. But because they may well point the way towards peace, Christian cultures of peace should encourage them.[16]

By asking questions. In the current global crisis, there is a war on terrorism which has no end in sight. There also is severe tension between the Islamic world and the West. Many people think they have the answers about how to handle this crisis. We in churches that are becoming cultures of peace also have our convictions. But it may be less important for us to state our convictions than to ask questions—which indicate that we are trying discern what God's word is in our time. Two questions seem to be especially important: What are our "enemies" saying? And what is God doing?

What are our "enemies" saying? Jesus tells his disciples, "But I say to you that listen, Love your enemies" (Luke 6:27). Jesus here is implying that he expects only some people to listen to him when he says "Love your enemies." His teaching will strike many people as odd. And Jesus knew that loving enemies means listening to them. We have seen, in chapter 4, that in our congregations we learn to "speak the truth" in love, and that this involves listening to the other's point of view, as well as speaking. We called this "double vision"—learning to see from the perspective of the other.

Listening to the person who is different from us—this is something that we Christians learn to do within our cultures of peace that we also want to do in the world. We will want to listen to the "realists"—secular and Christian realists—who think that "peacemakers" are unrealistic. That's why, for example, it's so important that we learn about the Just War theory.

We will also want to listen to our nation's enemies. How can Americans listen to the Iraqis, the Israelis to Palestinians, the Russians to the people of Chechnya? Americans may have a special problem here. A Church of England bishop who has been friendly to Anabaptists, the Rt. Rev. Peter Price, has said: "Americans don't listen." Is that true? How about citizens of other nations? Do they listen? Whatever our nationality, Jesus calls us to do what other people don't do—to love our enemies. We listen to those we love.

What is God doing? In a situation of polarization, enmity, and war, where is God at work? In Chapter One, we saw that in Jesus' day, God was at work among the Roman occupation army—in the person of the enemy, the Gentile soldier Cornelius. We also saw that God was building a new nation, miraculously calling the Galilean Jew Peter to make space in his world for the enemy Gentile centurion. Peter needed to discern whether this surprising connection was the work of God; so did the leaders of the church in Jerusalem.

In our time, it is fair to assume that God is at work among our enemies as well as among us, preparing them and us for reconciliations that will surprise everyone. In our day, where are the Peters and the Corneliuses? Where are the obscure, surprise connections taking place? These stirrings in individuals and surprise connections are signs of God at work, pointing towards God's goal of reconciling to himself all things (Colossians 1:20).

By offering hope. In many parts of our world today, hope is scarce. This may be especially true in the West. Bishop Lesslie Newbigin was a Scottish missionary who for many years was a leader in the Church of South India. After 40 years in India, he returned in the 1970s to Britain, where he served as minister of a small Reformed church in the city of Birmingham. Newbigin reports that he was often asked, "What is the greatest difficulty you face in moving from India to England?" He always answered, "The disappearance of hope."[17]

The civilization in the West today presents strong contrasts. There is unprecedented wealth, comfort, security, and protection against death and disease. There also is fear and hopelessness. Jesus would have predicted that: "The human life does not consist in the abundance of possessions" (Luke 12:15).

In our hopeless world, which spends money madly to bring security and happiness, Christian cultures of peace have little power. But we do have hope. It is not hope in success or in wealth or in our capacity to change everything. It is hope in God who will "gather up all things" in Jesus Christ (Ephesians 1:10).

Our hope is not an assurance that there will be no suffering, no tragedy. It is not a guarantee that Americans or Canadians can continue to live differently from everyone else in the world—in security and great wealth. But our hope is that God is at work in the midst of struggle and tragedy. The lives of individuals demonstrate this—people like Margarita whom God has pursued, forgiven, and saved from sin and disintegration, and given peace and new life in the "bond of peace" (Ephesians 4:3).

The Peters and the Corneliuses, enemies whom God has reconciled by his gracious work, also are signs of God's activity. We know that God's work tends not to be in the headlines. But God is at work on the margins, reticently but relentlessly. The numerical and spiritual growth of the Christian church around the world, amidst suffering and persecution, is a sign of God's work.

We also cherish the biblical hope that God will bring his mission to completeness. God's Kingdom will come; God's will will be done. Isaiah 11:6 offers us a vision of impossible reconciliation: "The wolf shall live with the lamb; the leopard shall lie down with the kid . . . and a little child shall lead them." The vision of Isaiah 19:23-25 seems at least as impossible—a reconciliation between "Egypt my people, and Assyria (Iraq) the work of my hands, and Israel my heritage." And of course the New Testament culminates in the vision of a great multitude "from every nation, from all tribes and peoples and languages," worshipping before God and the Lamb (Revelation 7:9). The destination of history is cosmic reconciliation.

Peace-church Christians will note the occasional signs in the political world that this is God's direction. We will recall the fall of the Berlin Wall without violence. We will remember the end of apartheid in South Africa without racial war. We will remember the end of Ferdinand Marcos' repressive dictatorship in the Philippines without the tanks shooting their guns. We will remember the transformation of the relationships that has brought some Jews and Palestinians, Irish Protestants and Catholics, Serbs and Bosnians, and others elsewhere, into a new realization of themselves as peaceful neighbors, even when the conflicts in their lands have not yet ended.

In these surprising events we will see signs of God's grace and God's will for all humanity. And we will praise God,

thanking him for these miraculous deeds, and expressing
our faith that the turmoil of this world may be the labor
pains of the renewed creation, in which all people will know
"the freedom of the glory of the children of God" (Romans
8:21).

9.
The Culture of Peace and Evangelism:
Offering Hope in Jesus

Christian congregations as "cultures of peace"—that sounds good. The gospel of peace is a satisfying way to understand the Bible, as well as the teaching and work of Jesus Christ. Its relevance to the behavior of individuals and groups in conflict is clear. Its contribution to the way people behave in their work is evident. But a nagging doubt remains. Can a church that is becoming a culture of peace grow?

In the era since "9/11" there appears to be endless war. In the Western media, it seems unnatural to talk about peace, and this is the case in other cultures as well. An ordinary American, Ethiopian, or Indonesian may find peace to be beautiful but somewhat unrealistic, and therefore to be a bit disconcerting—deeply to be desired but beyond our reach.

So we ask ourselves: Will churches that want to be cultures of peace find themselves to be small enclaves of idealists, perpetually ineffective and irrelevant?

While other churches grow, attracting new members, will churches that want to become cultures of peace stagnate, offending the experiences and values of people who might come to faith?

If we emphasize peace, will we be stumbling blocks to potential Christians?

Or is the opposite possible? Is peace "good news," as Peter said to Cornelius in Acts 10? We believe that it is. We believe that Jesus Christ and his peace are good news. We believe that, when churches preach the gospel of peace and attempt to apply it to all areas of life, God is at work, giving peace in its many dimensions. Further, we believe that when churches take peace seriously, God uses this as a way of attracting people to love Jesus Christ and to follow him in life.

The gospel of peace brings "peace with God." God's *shalom* is big; it is comprehensive. Peace is personal as well as interpersonal. Individuals whose lives are in disarray and who are rebelling against God are in deep trouble. They are trapped in sin. And God calls them to new life in Jesus Christ. God forgives their sins; God breaks the power of their bondages and addictions; God sets them free. And they experience "peace with God" (Romans 5:1).

Remember Margarita, whom we met in Chapter Three. When she "took Jesus into her heart . . . her whole life changed for the better." Her neighbors, accustomed to her erratic and violent behavior, "couldn't get over their surprise at the change in her life." Margarita used to be a violent, "undesirable neighbor," but now she knows the peace of God.[1] There is joy in the church and in the neighborhood. And, as Jesus informs us, There is "joy in heaven over one sinner who repents" (Luke 15:7).

All who come to new life embark on a journey. Jesus Christ—the "Prince of Peace"—is their traveling companion. Jesus promises never to leave us or forsake us (Matthew 28:20; Hebrews 13:5). He promises to lead us into all truth. So he will accompany us as God reveals to us new truths about the many facets of God's *shalom*.

Does each new convert begin the journey with the whole package of *shalom*? Most unlikely. But does the new believer have something that is a precious gift to those who have been Christians for a long time? Most certainly. S/he has a fresh experience of God's acceptance, and so s/he can share her/his faith with freshness and abandon. This freshness of faith is essential to the life of every church.

As the new believer matures as a Christian, s/he may discover the other facets of the peace-making life that we have described in this book: a passionate commitment to *shalom*, which brings justice and wholeness to all people, especially those who have been treated unjustly; forgiveness and reconciliation within the church, with skills and attitudes that spread out into all of life; peacemaking at work, in which Christians bring new ideas, expertise, and hope for unanticipated solutions to intractable problems.

The new Christian will join a community in which older Christians are also struggling with the whole package of *shalom*. As peacemakers, all of us are blessed (Matthew 5:9), but none of us is fully mature as a peacemaker. So the journey is for all of us, as we are transformed into the glory of the image of God, who is Jesus Christ (2 Corinthians 3:18).

So let us welcome new people into the community of peacemakers, which is the Church of Jesus Christ. Let us value the peacemakers in the church who have the gift of evangelism and are the midwives of new birth.

And let us receive people, just as they are, who are drawn to Christ. And what if the inquirers are soldiers? Some churches today face this issue and are working on appropriate responses. A particularly fascinating example comes from the Tidewater area of Virginia. This is one of the densest concentrations of military bases in the U.S., and it is also home to a cluster of Mennonite churches. How should they respond to military people who are attracted to their churches, in which God is at work, and in which they are attempting to be cultures of peace? How do they respond when, in the local economy, the military seems the only reliable source of jobs?

Together with the Virginia Mennonite Conference, the Tidewater churches between 1990 and 1995 pondered this and agreed to admit, as members, serving soldiers who "will sense a growing incompatibility between the military enterprise and the gosepl of peace." The hope is that they will "affirm loyalty to Jesus' teachings on peace, including his command to love enemies and to refrain from taking life." More recently the local churches appointed an ex-soldier to pioneer a program seeking "Alternatives to Military Careers."[2] In this, the Virginia Mennonites—in a missional situation—are doing something similar to the early church. Soldiers were attracted to life in Christ, and the third-century Christian leaders in Rome received them for catechesis; that is, for training in the Christian life in preparation for baptism. But they forbade them to kill.[3]

Although the peace church today, like the early church, says "no" to killing and war, the church that is becoming a culture of peace is not constantly talking about war. As its members walk on the journey of faith, they explore the many dimensions of *shalom*. All Christians, from the newest to the most venerable, have much to learn. As they make new discoveries, they find joy.

Members of peace churches are people saved by grace who have discovered fullness of life in Christ, and their dominant word is not "no" but "yes" (2 Corinthians 1:19-20). They are filled with faith, hope, commitment to justice, constructive imagination, resolute anticipation—and love. Peace churches are attractive.

The gospel of peace makes for abundant life. Throughout this book we have stated our conviction that when the gospel of peace is preached, believed, and applied to all areas of human life, people come to life. God sets individuals free from sin and oppression. God gives people new ideas and transforms their lives. And in many areas of their lives, people discover that Jesus the peacemaker has come so that "they may have life, and have it abundantly" (John 10:10). This attracts people.

Work. God opens the way to inventiveness and *shalom* in the world of work. This is one of the reasons why the Early Church grew despite persecution—because the gospel of Jesus Christ transformed people's working lives. Listen to Justin Martyr, a teacher in Rome who in 165 A.D. was executed for his faith by the imperial authorities. Writing to the emperor, Justin comments:

> Many who were once on your side have turned from the ways of violence and tyranny, overcome by observing the consistent lives of their neighbors, or noting the strange patience of their injured acquaintances, or experiencing the way they did business with them" (1 *Apology* 16).

The early Christians did business in a distinctive way that was just, patient, and peaceable. According to Justin, this led "many" to become Christians. Peacemaking Christians in business today can give similar testimonies of people who have come to faith through business practices that make *shalom*.

Local involvement. Peacemaking Christians respond in surprising ways to neighborhood tensions. In Boulder, Colorado, there is an area—"the hill"—that has often been a place of social protest and riots. One of the small groups in a local church decided to do something surprising. When a conflict was threatening to become a riot, they went to the hill and served delicious burritos to the "rainbow kids" whose presence was threatening.

On another occasion, when mayhem was brewing and the police were out in force with riot gear and guns, members of the church "walked the streets, talked to students, shopkeepers, and the police." Their pastor, Marilyn Miller, "went up to talk to the police about how they saw the situation . . . The police knew that we were from this church, and it was a great dialogue." The congregation by its presence and vision had helped a city find nonviolent solutions to conflict.[4]

This is a sample of the local *shalom*-making ministries of a peace church. But there are many more: programs to renew rundown housing, to tutor in schools, and to participate in neighborhood organizations, all of which are ways of seeking the *shalom* of the city (Jeremiah 29:7).[5] These attract people.

Peacemaking skills and experience. Over the past two thousand years, Christian churches have had a bad record of conflict—and outsiders have been repelled by Christians' destructive conflict. But today, Christians in peace churches are also growing as practical peacemakers. As we have indicated in Chapter Five, they are practicing the skills and attitudes of peacemaking. This can make their life attractive and contagious.

Through the work of Christian mediators, some churches which have known fracture and division have experienced reconciliation. They can testify: "Yes, we have known broken relations; we, like other people, have had bad conflict. But Jesus Christ is alive, and he can do miraculous things. He has healed our community by teaching us how to have good conflict. Jesus Christ is the reconciler. Do you want to experience that in your lives?"

This experience of peacemaking, as well as the development of skills and attitudes of peacemaking, can lead to a life of wholeness and genuineness that is deeply attractive. Canon Robert Warren is one of England's leading authorities on evangelism. Over many years he has learned that authenticity—and practical peacemaking—are at the heart of church growth.

Despite the forces at work which seem to have marginalized the church, we stand today faced with a great new opportunity to speak the good news of Christ into our culture by the way we live that truth in the life of the local church . . . There are hungers in our society that make the life of the church at least potentially of great significance . . . There is a great hunger for relationships today . . . There is also a great hunger for demonstration today . . . People want to see whether it works. The church is called to be the pilot project of the new humanity established by Christ . . . . Not least is the world looking for models of handling conflict . . . Conflicts in the church can seem such a distraction from getting on with the real work; but *this is the real work.* When people come near such a community they will instinctively know how real the relationships are.[6]

The culture of peace embodies shalom *"before the watching world."* Of course, churches that are becoming cultures of peace do not live a *shalom* vision perfectly. They are marred by sin, and they live their vision incompletely. So they always need to be modest and repentant. Nevertheless, the church has an extraordinary calling. Jesus said of his gathered disciples, "You are the light of the world . . . [You are] a city built on a hill" (Matthew 5:14). The church is meant to live now in the way that God wants everyone to live. The church is meant to be a demonstration of God's intent for the whole world. The church is "the preview community."[7] It is to be a community that is visible, "the sign and foretaste of God's reign of justice, freedom, and love."[8] As Mennonite theologian John Howard Yoder put it, the church lives its life "before the watching world."[9]

In September and October, 2004—10 years after the massacres of Rwanda—the Issue Group on Reconciliation of the Forum on World Evangelization of the Lausanne Committee on World Evangelization met in Pattya, Thailand. Its message to the churches around the world is profound:

> The church itself ought to be a key indication of hope, a living alternative, infusing and challenging the social sphere with a more radical vision of God's reconciliation. Examples of the church visibly living the alternative include: across long-divided lines, Christians form holy friendships, offer hospitality, share meals, pray, and read Scripture together, celebrate holy communion, mutually confess and forgive, and forge common mission; unlearn habits of superiority, inferiority, and separation; celebrate together, and praise and worship God while engaging the world's pain and working towards *shalom*; free Christian institutions of discrimination and unjust use of resources; show remarkable joy amidst difficult work; marry across ethnic boundaries and divided lines, with blended families becoming a sign of a new community. At the heart of the church's alternative witness is the birth and perseverance of blended congregations where historically separated peoples share deep, common life.[10]

Some people will be offended by the vision of the church as a culture of peace. Some people won't like what they see. Some non-Christians view all Christians as soft-headed and romantic. They will dismiss the gospel of peace as unrealistic.

Some Christians will be similarly unimpressed. Preaching "the gospel of peace"—this can't be a proper use of the

Bible! Many Christians have a deeply felt and unexamined sense of emotional identification with their nation. By comparison, their identification with Jesus Christ and his global body is theoretical and emotionally tepid. For these reasons, some people—both non-Christians and Christians—will never join a church that is becoming a culture of peace, unless God gives them a special experience that changes their empathies and reflexes. If we start applying the gospel of peace more consistently to all areas of life, we could even have problems in our own congregations. Some of our members might be alarmed by new aspects of Jesus' good news, leave the church, and join another Christian tradition in which peace is not on the agenda.

Missionaries have been cautious about mentioning peace. So should we, therefore, in the interest of keeping our members or getting new ones, stop talking about peace? Missionaries from peace churches at times have kept peace, even in conflict-laden situations, at the heart of their evangelistic activity.[11] But often they have offered peace only as a personal matter. They have presented God's desire for peace with the individual, forgiven sinners, as primary. This, they have said, is the heart of the gospel. Other dimensions of peace they have regarded as secondary—peripheral, supplemental, desirable, to be sure, but less important than the "gospel."

Sometimes missionaries from churches whose theologies have emphasized peace have been embarrassed by their churches' approach to war, or afraid that peace would offend potential converts.[12] This is understandable: the Bible's approach to many issues, including violence and conflict, is "foolishness" which contradicts normal human wisdom. But the biblical writers offer it as "the power of God and the wisdom of God" (1 Corinthians 1:21-24).

In Acts 10, Peter and Cornelius together discovered the surprising meaning of the "good news of peace" which Jesus had brought. It led, to Peter's astonishment, to Jews and Gentiles—clean and unclean, oppressed and oppressors—becoming brothers and sisters, one in baptism, one in the Holy Spirit. The Acts 10 story shows us how the gospel of peace subverts and upends the conventional way of viewing the world. It also shows us that mission and peace are synergistic.

When the General Council of the Mennonite World Conference met in Guatemala in 2000, I (Paulus) was interested in the discussion on global mission. It was an interesting scene. When less affluent Christians spoke, it was clear that they were not hampered by a split between peace and mission. They could easily go back and forth between the mission realm and the peace realm. They could discuss the church's mission in the same breath as racism, street children, hunger, prostitution, and war. In the hearts and minds of these people there was no division between the soul and the body. For them, the gospel of Jesus Christ addresses both body and soul.

When more affluent Christians spoke, however, their speeches implied a dichotomy between mission and peace, as if the two were separate entities pitted against each other. So we must ask: where does this separation between mission and peace come from? Does it come from the gospel? Or does it come from an affluent mindset?

If missionaries omit peace, they deprive the new converts. And the consequences can be terrible. Consider the experience of Rwanda, "one of Africa's most evangelized nations." It is now famed, not for its faith, but for its massacres. In three months of 1994, approximately 800,000 people were killed. "The fighting was hand-to-hand, intimate, and unspeakable, a kind of bloodlust that left those who managed to escape it hollow-eyed and mute."[13]

How could Christians do this kind of thing to other people, even to other Christians? Was their behavior related to the failure of many missionaries to preach the gospel of peace and to teach that in Christ there is unity between members of different tribes? But there is another Rwandan story—the story of the East African Revival Fellowship whose participants, both African and Western, discovered the deep meaning of "Calvary's love for all, particularly those who are persecuting you." In the intra-tribal bloodletting which wracked Rwanda, the Revival brothers were often the first ones to be attacked. In the massacres, an estimated 50,000 brothers were killed. As missionary theologian David W. Shenk has commented,

[These people] did not and would not hate or kill. They were the people of the Lamb, Jesus, who, even in his crucifixion, forgave his enemies. The witness of these Christians who have lived and proclaimed forgiveness in Jesus Christ . . . [is that] the Way of Jesus is the only real hope for the healing of the Rwandan nation.[14]

That is why the Issue Group on Reconciliation of the Lausanne Committee on World Evangelization has issued the following as the first of its seven "conclusions and recommendations." Christian churches should

embrace biblically holistic reconciliation at the heart of the gospel and Christian life and mission in the 21st century, and as integral to evangelism and justice.[15]

Jesus and numbers. On one occasion, the evangelist Luke records, when "large crowds were traveling with him," Jesus turned to them and said (Luke 14:25-27):

Whoever comes to me and does not hate father and mother, wife and children, brothers and sisters, yes, and even life itself, cannot be my disciple. Whoever does not carry the cross and follow me cannot be my disciple.

Jesus told the crowds not what they wanted to hear, and not what would build the largest possible movement; he told them what he knew they needed to hear. Jesus loved people and wanted them to follow him, but he cared about the authenticity of their lives more than he cared about numbers.

In a similar passage in the gospel of John, Jesus gave his disciples teaching that they found off-putting. They said, "This teaching is difficult: who can accept it?" For this reason, "many of his disciples turned back and no longer went about with him." So what did Jesus do? Did he drop his difficult message? John reports that Jesus asked his 12 closest disciples, "Do you also wish to go away?" Peter's response was heartfelt: "Lord, to whom can we go? You have the words of eternal life. We have come to believe and know that you are the Holy One of God" (John 6:60ff).

From Jesus and his first disciples we can learn this: numerical growth is important. God wants everybody to be saved (1 Timothy 2:4). And Jesus wants his disciples to join him in seeking for those who are lost (Luke 15:3-7). But people will not find life in Jesus if they ignore his teachings, which are "the words of eternal life" (John 6:68).

English evangelical theologian/statesman John Stott has repeatedly stated his concern about the contemporary state of the worldwide church: "One of the biggest problems in the church today is growth without depth.[16] The Issue Group on Reconciliation of the Lausanne Committee on World Evangelization has recently identified numerous "ideologies of escape" that Christians must reject. These ideologies steer the church away from its true mission. One of these ideologies is:

Adopting numbers of conversions or church plants as a primary measure of Christianity's growth, allowing churches or ministries to grow with superficial discipleship, homogeneously, or in ways that perpetuate histories and systems of separation and alienation. This tacit approval of permanent boundaries and segregated lives limited to "people like us" falsely blesses the chasm between alienated groups and disables our ability to be self-critical.[17]

Again, the Issue Group on Reconciliation says:

In too many cases, Christians have been implicated in destructive conflict which has overtaken vast areas of revival and church-planting. The church has failed to be self-critical or discerning enough, or to adequately answer, "How did this happen, and where did Christians fail?"[18]

So let us introduce people to Jesus and his way of peace confidently and with hope. Jesus is good news, not when we edit and expurgate and prettify him, but as the New Testament evangelists present him. Let us follow him and offer him to the world—difficult sayings and all. And God will take care of the numbers.

New people will be attracted to churches that are cultures of peace. The gospel of peace is gospel. It is good news! It makes a life-giving difference to people. All over the world, people are attracted to the peace churches because Jesus is the "way, the truth, and the life" (John 14:6). His way, unlike the dominant values of our time, is one of abundant life.

In any congregation that is becoming a culture of peace, there will be stories of people who have been attracted to faith in Jesus Christ because his news is good, and because he sets people free from many bondages, including the bondages of injustice and violence. When people are "in Christ," they are free indeed.

Every church that is becoming a culture of peace has stories of people who have been drawn to join them because they take the gospel of peace seriously and attempt to live it. At times, these are people who have found Jesus attractive but have had doubts about the Christian Church, which seems complicit with violence and injustice. These people often have a deep longing for an authentic life, for a life that rings true. Jesus and his way of peace make sense to them in a way that dominant cultural values, and the values of other religions, do not make sense.

Arthur Paul Boers, who for 16 years was a pastor in Canada, recently commented: "In every church I served as pastor, it was precisely our commitment to the gospel, our lifting high of God's priorities of peace and justice on earth as in heaven, that brought people through our doors."[19]

The attraction of people to Jesus the Prince of Peace and to churches that are committed to peace is happening all over the world. This is one reason why the growing global Anabaptist family is increasingly finding its common identity to be a peace church.[20]

The gospel of peace makes a difference in people's lives. It is worth sharing. More than that, we are selfish if we don't share it. Jesus has given us truth to share with others. It is truth that can be lived; it works in real life. Our calling is to show, in our churches and friendships and jobs and families, that the gospel of peace is practical.

Unlike the way of the world, this is a way of wisdom. When the rains fall, floods rise, and winds blow, other houses will collapse, but a house built on Jesus and his teaching will stand (Matthew 7:24-27). It is our privilege to attract and invite people to Jesus and his way of wisdom and truth, so that they may join us in abundant living.

Jesus is the church's main attraction. In many parts of the world there are people who find the Christian Church to be bad news: Christianity is predictable; it is risk-adverse; it is boring. Many people associate the church with violence— the Crusades of the Middle Ages, the religious wars of early modern Europe, the "troubles" between Protestants and Catholics in Northern Ireland, the war in Iraq in the twenty-first century. The Christian Church must face the fact: all over the world people reject Christianity because of Christians' terrible record of violence.

Christians have offered worship to Jesus but paid no attention to what he said. At the end of his Sermon on the Mount, Jesus expressed his concern—that many people would call him, "Lord, Lord," and ignore his teaching (Matthew 7:21). Repeatedly, in the history of global Christianity, Jesus' concern has been borne out. So a primary goal of Christian leaders today, in many settings, must not be outreach, but what spiritual writer Dallas Willard calls "inreach"—preparing to "understand clearly what it means to be a disciple of Jesus and to be solidly committed to discipleship in their whole life. That is, when asked who they are, the first words out of their mouth would be, 'I am an apprentice of Jesus Christ.'"[21]

Inreach, in which Christians become apprentices of Jesus Christ, might have a significant effect upon the Christian Church globally. In many parts of the world people are intrigued by Jesus. His person is winsome, his story is compelling, his teachings make sense. And when people find Christians who love Jesus and take his teachings so seriously that they apply them to all areas of their lives, people are astonished, delighted, and attracted. Their journeys to faith are not always quick. But when they see Jesus' way embodied in communities of faith—when they see churches that are becoming cultures of peace—they are willing to consider giving their lives to the One who gave his life for them.

Before we close, let us recall Jesus' temptations in the wilderness (Matthew 4:1-11). In the story of his baptism (Matthew 3:16-17) which precedes his temptations, Jesus receives his inauguration as the "Son of God." The question underlying the wilderness testing is "What qualifies Jesus as the Son of God?" This is why the devil keeps questioning Jesus with an *if* clause: "*If* you *are* the Son of God" (Matthew 4:3 and 6). The devil questions the legitimacy of the heavenly voice that said of Jesus, "This is my Son, the beloved." The devil challenges Jesus to prove that he is indeed the Son of God.

But what kind of proof does the devil ask Jesus to provide? He demands a *show of force*—to command the stones to become loaves of bread, to throw himself down from the pinnacle of the temple, and to acquire all the kingdoms of the world and their splendor. This is the proof that the world knows best. If you claim a certain title, you have to show a force commensurate to the title.

But Jesus refuses to prove his sonship by a show of force. He points to a different way. Jesus knows it is not force but spirit which legitimates and reveals that he is God's son. This is the spirit that animates Jesus' Beatitudes and pulses through Jesus' Sermon on the Mount (Matthew 5-7)—a spirit of sonship.

Who, in Jesus' seventh beatitude, are the children of God? It is not those who wield force, but the "peacemakers" (Matthew 5:9).

The way to life, Jesus tells us, is a narrow way. It can be hard and many will miss it (Matthew 7:14). But with joy we Christians can testify: the way of peace is the way of life. It is the gift of Jesus who has come that we "may have life, and have it abundantly" (John 10:10). We have discovered, to our grateful delight, that Jesus has transformed our lives. He has changed the way we live and think and work. He is good. He is authentic. He is attractive. And people want to join him on the way of peace.

APPENDIX I:
Agreeing and Disagreeing in Love

"Making every effort to maintain the unity of the Spirit in the bond of peace" (Ephesians 4:3), as both individual members and the body of Christ, we pledge that we shall:

IN THOUGHT _____

Accept conflict
1. Acknowledge together that conflict is a normal part of our life in the church. *Romans 14:1-8, 10-12, 17-19, 15:1-7*

Affirm hope
2. Affirm that as God walks with us in conflict, we can work through to growth. *Ephesians 4:15-16*

Commit to prayer
3. Admit our needs and commit ourselves to pray for a mutually satisfactory solution (no prayers for my success or for the other to change but to find a joint way).
James 5:16

IN ACTION _____

Go to the other . . .
4. Go directly to those with whom we disagree; avoid behind-the-back criticism.* *Matthew 5:23-24; 18:15-20*

. . . In the spirit of humility
5. Go in gentleness, patience, and humility. Place the problem between us at neither doorstep and own our part in the conflict instead of pointing out the others'.
Galatians 6:1-5

Be quick to listen

6. Listen carefully, summarize and check out what is heard before responding. Seek as much to understand as to be understood. *James 1:19; Proverbs 18:13*

Be slow to judge

7. Suspend judgments, avoid labeling, end name calling, discard threats and act in a nondefensive, nonreactive way. *Romans 2:1-4; Galatians 5:22-26*

Be willing to negotiate

8. Work through the disagreements constructively. *Acts 15; Philippians 2:1-11*

- Identify issues, interests, and needs of both (rather than take positions).

- Generate a variety of options for meeting both parties' needs (rather than defending one's own way).

- Evaluate options by how they meet the needs and satisfy the interests of all sides (not one side's values).

- Collaborate in working out a joint solution (so both sides gain, both grow and win).

- Cooperate with the emerging agreement (accept the possible, not demand your ideal).

- Reward each other for each step forward, toward agreement (celebrate mutuality).

IN LIFE
Be steadfast in love
9. Be firm in our commitment to seek a mutual solution; be stubborn in holding to our common foundation in Christ; be steadfast in love. *Colossians 3:12-15*

Be open to mediation
10. Be open to accept skilled help. If we cannot reach agreement among ourselves, we will use those with gifts and training in mediation in the larger church. *Philippians 4:1-3*

Trust the community
11. We will trust the community, and if we cannot reach agreement or experience reconciliation, we will turn the decision over to others in the congregation or from the broader church. *Acts 15*

   - In one-to-one or small group disputes, this may mean allowing others to arbitrate.

   - In congregational, conference district, or denominational disputes, this may mean allowing others to arbitrate or implementing constitutional decision-making processes, insuring that they are done in the spirit of these guidelines, and abiding by whatever decision is made.

Be the Body of Christ
12. Believe in and rely on the solidarity of the Body of Christ and its commitment to peace and justice, rather than resort to the courts of law. *1 Corinthians 6:1-6*

Christians are not immune to conflict. We face it in our homes and churches, in our neighborhoods and work places. Wherever we interact with other people, we experience conflict.

Too often conflict becomes destructive because we try to avoid it, or because we don't know how to face it well. But we can make it an opportunity to grow, to become more faithful to Jesus, to model Christ-like love for one another.

To work constructively with conflict, we need skills. "Agreeing and Disagreeing in Love" outlines approaches to conflict that will help us live out our calling to be Christian peacemakers.

BIBLICAL FOUNDATION

The Bible guides us to seek reconciliation when we disagree. Scripture teaches us that conflict can be an arena for God's revelation.

- Reconciliation is at the heart of the gospel. Through Christ we are reconciled to God, who gives us the ministry of reconciliation. *Romans 5:1-11; 2 Corinthians 5:17-20*

- Reconciliation with others in the church is a prelude to genuine worship. *Matthew 5:23-24*

- Jesus describes a process for addressing conflict and restoring relationships in the church. *Matthew 18:15-22*

- Groups in the early church came together to talk about their differences, to seek the Spirit's leading as they worked for consensus. *Acts 6:1-6; Acts 15:1-3*

- The church needs each person's gifts and perspectives; no one has a corner on truth. *1 Corinthians 12-14*

- God's chosen ones are to bear with one another, to forgive each other, and to clothe themselves "with love, which binds everything together in perfect harmony." *Colossians 3:12-17*

- We are to grow in unity and maturity by speaking the truth in love. *Ephesians 4:1-16*

- God calls us to act and speak with respect for each other despite differences of culture or conviction. *Romans 14:1-7; James 1:19; John 7:51; Ephesians 4:25-32; Matthew 7:1-5; 1 Peter 3:8,16*

- God's people do not seek the absence of conflict but the presence of shalom, a peace based on justice. *Amos 5:21-24, Micah 6:6-8; Isaiah 58; Matthew 23:23-24; Luke 4:18-19*

ADOPTING THE GUIDELINES

We encourage congregations, area conferences, church boards, and agencies to adopt the guidelines for agreeing and disagreeing in love, and to use them. The process you use to consider adopting the guidelines can itself be a model for working through differences together.

Design a process to study the guidelines and decide whether to adopt them. Your written process design could includes these pieces:

A. Define the issue: Should our group adopt these guidelines?

B. Identify goals: To enhance our commitment and ability to deal constructively with conflict. (Add your goals.)

C. Clarify steps and timeline:

1. Approve the process design. The appropriate decision-making body acts to do this.

2. Study the guidelines and the biblical foundations.

a. Offer a Sunday school class on conflict resolution skills for congregations.

    b. Invite an outside resource person to present a
       Saturday workshop on the topic.

    c. Encourage committees and small groups to study
       the guidelines.

3. Talk together about using the guidelines.

    a. Discuss ways to use the guidelines in your context.

    b. Integrate the guidelines into constitutions, bylaws,
       personnel policies.

    c. Note concerns that arise and work to resolve them.

4. Implement the decision rule (see immediately below).

D. State the decision rule: Identify who will make the decision, and how it will be made.

USING THE GUIDELINES

After your group has adopted the guidelines, you can:

- Display the "Agreeing and Disagreeing in Love" poster in rooms where committees meet.

- Include training on the guidelines in new member classes or orientation sessions.

- Use reconciliation and conflict resolution as a focus for worship from time to time.

- Include articles in your newsletter about the guidelines and your experience with them.

- Appoint a process observer for your meetings, to monitor your group's use of the guidelines.

- Every year evaluate how your group is working with conflict.

SEVERAL CAUTIONS

The guidelines should not be used as a substitute for the proper exercise of authority. When laws have been broken or people abused, mediation would be appropriate only at later stages, when offenders have take responsibility for their actions and victims are requesting face-to-face meetings as a step toward their own healing.

The guidelines may inform disciplinary or grievance procedures, but they are not intended to be a substitute for such procedures. In cross-cultural settings, the guidelines should be adapted to fit the context.

SOME BASIC PRINCIPLES

In interpersonal and group conflicts, people can take many of the steps identified in the guidelines without the help of an impartial third party. But when conflict escalates and the principal parties cannot resolve it by negotiating together, they should seek outside help.

In mediation, disputing parties come to their own agreement with the assistance of an objective third party. Those serving as mediators should be trained; attempting to mediate a dispute without having the necessary skills can make matters worse. Trained mediators can help people come to agreement on issues and also aid in healing broken relationships.

If mediation fails to resolve a dispute, arbitration could be sought. The disputing parties would agree in advance to abide by whatever decision the arbitrators make. The arbitrators listen to each party's case, consult with each other, and agree on a win-win decision that attempts to address the interests of all the parties.

INFORMATION

For more information contact:

Mennonite Church USA—Peace Advocate;
Peace@MennoniteUSA.org; Toll-free 866-866-2872,
www.MennoniteUSA.org/peace

Lombard Mennonite Peace Center—101 W. 22nd Street,
Suite 206, Lombard, IL 60148; 630-627-0507;
Admin@LMPeaceCenter.org; www.LMPeaceCenter.org

Mennonite Conciliation Service—21 South 12th St., PO Box
500, Akron, PA 17501-0500; 717-859-3889; mcs@mccus.org;
www.mcc.org/us/peaceandjustice/mcs.html

*Go directly if you are European-North American; in other cultures disagreements are often addressed through a trusted go-between.

APPENDIX II:
The Just War Theory

A presumption binds all Christians: Christians should do no harm to their neighbors; how they treat their enemies is the key test of whether they love their neighbors; the possibility of taking even one human life is a "prospect we should consider in fear and trembling." But a "just" or "limited" war is justifiable, despite the strong presumption against it, if certain criteria for its origins and conduct are met.

1. JUST CAUSE: before war breaks out

- There must be a *just cause:* "a real and certain danger," to protect innocent life, to preserve conditions necessary for decent human existence, to secure basic human rights.

- The war must be declared by a *competent authority,* not by a private group or individuals.

- The warring parties must recognize the *comparative justice* of their causes; no state should act on the basis that it has "absolute justice" on its side.

- There must be a *right intention;* there must be no ulterior motive.

- The war must be a *last resort;* all peaceful alternatives must have been exhausted.

- There must be a *probability of success,* which prevents an irrational resort to force or hopeless resistance.

- There must be *proportionality:* the destruction to be inflicted and the costs incurred by the war must be proportionate to the good expected by taking up arms.

2. JUST MEANS: as the war is prosecuted, its conduct remains under continuous scrutiny.

- The means must be *discriminate*: this prohibits intentional attacks on non-combatants and non-military targets, and condemns "total war."

- The means must be *proportionate*: destruction caused by actions in war must be proportionate to the good expected by the actions.

Based upon *The Challenge of Peace: God's Promise and Our Response*, A Pastoral Letter on War and Peace, National Conference of Catholic Bishops, USA (United States Catholic Conference, 1983), sections 80-110.

Endnotes

Introduction

1 Alan Kreider, "Is a Peace Church Possible?"; "Is a Peace Church Possible? The Church's 'Domestic' Life"; "Is a Peace Church Possible? The Church's 'Foreign Policy'—Worship"; "Is a Peace Church Possible? The Church's 'Foreign Policy'—Work, War, Witness," in *Anabaptism Today*, issues 19-22 (1998-1999).

2 London: New Ground, 2000.

3 John Paul II, encyclical *Evangelium vitae [Gospel of Life]* (1995): http://www.vatican.va/edocs/ENG0141/INDEX.HTM; Elise Boulding, *Cultures of Peace: The Hidden Side of History* (Syracuse, NY: Syracuse University Press, 2000); Fernando Enns, Scott Holland, and Ann Riggs, eds., *Seeking Cultures of Peace: A Peace Church Conversation* (Telford, PA: Cascadia Publishing House, 2004).

4 Clifford Geertz, *The Interpretation of Cultures: Selected Essays* (New York: Basic Books, 1973), 5.

5 Paul S. Fiddes, "The Story and the Stories: Revelation and the Challenge of Postmodern Culture," in Paul S. Fiddes, ed., *Faith in the Centre: Christianity and Culture* (Oxford: Regent's Park College, with Macon, GA: Smyth & Helwys, 2001), 77.

Chapter 1

1 Justin Martyr, *Dialogue with Trypho* 110.2-3.

2 Irenaeus, *Adv. Haer* 4.34.4; Tertullian, *Adv. Marc.* 3.21; Origen, *Contra Celsum* 5.33; *Didascalia Apostolorum* 6.5.

3 Willard Swartley, *Covenant of Peace: Restoring the Neglected Peace in New Testament Theology and Ethics* (Grand Rapids: Eerdmans, 2006).

4 Eusebius, *Ecclesiastical History* 2.25.6.

Chapter 2

1 Marlin E. Miller, "The Gospel of Peace," in Robert Ramseyer, ed., *Mission and the Peace Witness* (Scottdale, PA: Herald Press, 1979), 9-23.

2 Andrew Walls, "From Christendom to World Christianity," in *The Cross-Cultural Process in Christian History* (Maryknoll, NY: Orbis Books, 2002), 49-71.

3 Dietrich Bonhoeffer, *Ethics*, trans. Neville Horton Smith (New York: Simon & Schuster, 1995), 244-245.

4 Miroslav Volf, *Exclusion and Embrace: A Theological Exploration of Identity, Otherness, and Reconciliation* (Nashville: Abingdon Press, 1996), 129.

5 David P. Barash, *Introduction to Peace Studies* (Belmont, CA: Wadsworth Publishing Company, 1991), 7-8.

6 Johan Galtung, *Peace By Peaceful Means: Peace and Conflict, Development and Civilization* (Oslo: PRIO International Peace Research Institute and London: SAGE Publications, 1996), 9.

7 Ulrich Mauser, *The Gospel of Peace: A Scriptural Message For Today's World* (Louisville, KY: Westminster/John Knox Press, 1992), 13.

8 Perry Yoder, *Shalom: The Bible's Word for Salvation, Justice, and Peace* (Newton, KS: Faith and Life Press, 1987), 10-16; see also Walter Brueggemann, *Living Toward A Vision: Biblical Reflections on Shalom* (New York: United Church Press, 1976), 18-20.

9 For a profound reflection on *shalom* as it impacts an inner-city community, see Mark R. Gornik, *To Live in Peace: Biblical Faith and the Changing Inner City* (Grand Rapids: Eerdmans, 2002), chapter 3.

10 Ibid., 101.

11 Justin Martyr, *Dialogue with Trypho* 110.2-3.

12 H. Richard Niebuhr, *The Social Sources of Denominationalism* (New York: Henry Holt and Co., 1929), 281-283.

13 Ibid., 283-284.

14 John Warkentin, in a report from Dalton Reimer, Peace Education Commission of the United States Conference of Mennonite Brethren Churches to the Peace Council of the Mennonite World Conference, January 25, 2003.

Chapter 3

1 Report to the Peace Council of Mennonite World Conference from Convención de Iglesias Evangélicas Menonitas de Nicaragua (CIEMN, the Mennonite Church in Nicaragua), 2003.

2 Pastor Pascal Misakabu Nzala, Report to the Peace Council, Mennonite World Conference, March 2003.

3 Shet Sonwani, Report to the Peace Council, Mennonite World Conference, Bihar Mennonite Mandali, October 24, 2002.

4 Report to the Peace Council, Mennonite World Conference, from Persatuan Gereja-Gereja Kristen Muria Indonesia (GKMI), 2003.

5 Rev. Fimbo Ganvunze, Report to the Peace Council, Mennonite World Conference, March 28, 2003.

6 Walter Wink, *Engaging the Powers: Discernment and Resistance in a World of Domination* (Minneapolis: Fortress Press, 1992), 13ff.

7 Gerhard Lohfink, "'Schwerter zu Pflugscharen': Die Rezeption von Jes 2, 1-5 par Mi 4, 1-5 in der Alten Kirche und im Neuen Testament," *Theologische Quartalschrift* 166 (1986): 184-209 surveys the use of the Isaiah and Micah passages in early Christian writers and notes their absence in Augustine.

8 Augustine, *Enarr. in ps.* 45.10. See also *Enarr. in ps.* 48.17.

9 Menno Simons, *The New Birth* (1537), in J.C. Wenger and Leonard

Verduin, eds., *Complete Works of Menno Simons* (Scottdale, PA: Herald Press,1956), 94.

Chapter 4

1 See Joseph Liechty, "Why Did Dirk Willems Turn Back? Examining Motives for Nonviolent Love," *Anabaptism Today* 6 (June 1994), 7-12.

2 Philip P. Hallie, *Lest Innocent Blood Be Shed: The Story of the Village of Le Chambon and How Goodness Happened There* (New York: Harper & Row, 1979), 9, 180; David P. Gushee, *The Righteous Gentiles of the Holocaust: A Christian Interpretation* (Minneapolis: Fortress Press, 1994), 136-137, 144.

3 Aristotle, *Ethics*, 1179b25-26, found in Stanley Hauerwas, *A Community of Character: Toward a Constructive Christian Social Ethic* (Notre Dame: University of Notre Dame Press, 1981), 137.

4 William Fleming and Chas. P. Krauth, *The Vocabulary of Philosophy: Mental, Moral, and Metaphysical* (Philadelphia: Smith, English and Co., 1860), 549.

5 Nancey Murphy, "Using MacIntyre's Method in Christian Ethics," in *Virtues and Practices in the Christian Tradition: Christian Ethics after MacIntyre*, ed. Nancey Murphy, Brad J. Kallenberg, and Mark Thiessen Nation (Harrisburg, PA: Trinity Press International, 1997), 40.

6 Rodney Clapp, *A Peculiar People: The Church as Culture in a Post-Christian Society* (Downers Grove, IL: InterVarsity Press, 1996).

7 The first and third of these expressions come from Reinhold Niebuhr, the second from M. Scott Peck. See Reinhold Niebuhr, *The Nature and Destiny of Man*, Vol. I: *Human Nature*, Library of Theological Ethics, reprint edition (Louisville, KY: Westminster John Knox Press, 1996), 152, 154-156; M. Scott Peck, *The Different Drum: Community Making and Peace*, Touchtone Book, second Touchtone edition (New York: Simon and Schuster, 1998), 179; Reinhold Niebuhr, *The Essential Reinhold Niebuhr*, ed. Robert McAfee Brown (New Haven and London: Yale University Press, 1986), 63.

8 Stanley Hauerwas, *The Peaceable Kingdom: A Primer in Christian Ethics* (London: SCM Press, 1984), 99.

9 Gerhard Lohfink, *Jesus and Community: The Social Dimension of Christian Faith* (London: SPCK, 1985), 122.

10 *Independent* (an English daily newspaper), 6 September 1995. Another metaphor for the church as a place where the craft of living is "workshop" in which "apprenticeship" is taking place, which is where we "learn the craft of peacemaking" (L. Gregory Jones, *Embodying Forgiveness: A Theological Analysis* [Grand Rapids: Eerdmans, 1995]).

11 Our treatment of Matthew 18:15-20 owes much to Stanley Hauerwas, "Peacemaking: The Virture of the Church," in his *Christian Exis-*

tence Today: Essays on Church, World, and Living Between (Durham, NC: The Labyrinth Press, 1988), 89-97; and John H. Yoder, "Practicing the Rule of Christ," in *Virtues and Practices in the Christian Tradition: Christian Ethics after MacIntyre*, ed. Nancey Murphy, Brad J. Kallenberg, and Mark Thiessen Nation (Harrisburg, PA: Trinity Press International, 1997), 132-160.

12 Some biblical manuscripts add "against you."

13 David Augsburger, *Pastoral Counseling across Cultures* (Philadelphia: Westminster Press: 1986).

14 Matthew 18:17; the one other time Jesus uses *ekklesia* is Matthew 16:18.

Chapter 5

1 John Paul Lederach, *Journey Toward Reconciliation* (Scottdale, PA: Herald Press, 1999), 101.

2 Carolyn Schrock-Shenk and Lawrence Ressler, *Making Peace with Conflict: Practical Skills for Conflict Transformation* (Scottdale, PA: Herald Press, 1999), 26-27.

3 Carolyn Schrock-Shenk, ed., *Mediation and Facilitation Training Manual: Foundations and Skills for Constructive Conflict Transformation*, 4th ed. (Akron, PA: Mennonite Conciliation Service, 2000), 27.

4 Ron Kraybill, "From Head to Heart: The Cycle of Reconciliation," in Schrock-Shenk, *Mediation and Facilitation Training Manual*, 31-34.

5 Arthur Paul Boers, *Never Call Them Jerks: Healthy Responses to Difficult Behavior* (Bethesda, MD: Alban Institute, 1999).

6 We all too easily forget that speaking the truth involves the positive truth as well as the negative.

7 Miroslav Volf, *Exclusion and Embrace: A Theological Exploration of Identity, Otherness, and Reconciliation* (Nashville: Abingdon Press, 1996), 213, 250-253.

8 Gerald W. Schlabach,"Patterns of Church Life, 1," *The Mennonite* (September 15, 1998), 8-9.

9 Stanley Hauerwas and William H. Willimon, *Resident Aliens: Life in the Christian Colony* (Nashville, TN: Abingdon Press, 1990), 102.

10 Craig Dykstra, *Vision and Character: A Christian Education Alternative to Kohlberg* (New York: Paulist Press, 1981), 66.

11 Hauerwas and Willimon, *Resident Aliens*, 97.

12 Mark R. Gornick, *To Live in Peace: Biblical Faith and the Changing Inner City* (Grand Rapids: Eerdmans, 2002), 103-105.

13 For practical suggestions and wise advice about decision-making, see Chapter 5 of Schrock-Shenk, ed., *Mediation and Facilitation Training Manual*, 205-234; also Alastair McKay, "Congregational Decision Making," in Schrock-Shenk and Ressler, *Making Peace with Conflict*, 177-187. For a more theological exposition see Luke T. Johnson,

Scripture and Discernment: Decision Making in the Church (Nashville, Abingdon Press, 1996).

14 John H. Yoder, *For The Nations: Essays Evangelical and Public* (Grand Rapids, MI: Eerdmans, 1997), 186; see also 177, 233-234; idem, *Body Politics: Five Practices of the Christian Community Before the Watching World* (Scottdale, PA: Herald Press, 2001), 2.

15 Yoder, *For the Nations*, 177.

16 Hauerwas and Willimon, *Resident Aliens*, 78.

17 Gerard Hughes, *In Search of a Way: Two Journeys of Discovery* (Rome and Sydney: E.J. Dwyer, 1978), 75.

Chapter 6

1 Richard R. Gaillardetz, *Transforming Our Days: Spirituality, Community and Liturgy in the Technological Culture* (New York: Crossroad, 2000), 120.

2 E.g., the deacon Sanctus who, during the persecution in Lyons in Gaul in 177, replied to every question, "I am a Christian." Herbert Musurillo, *The Acts of the Christian Martyrs* (Oxford: Clarendon Press, 1972), 69.

3 J. Nelson Kraybill, "A Christian Pledge of Allegiance," *The Mennonite*, August 3, 2004, 9-11. The second theologian is June Alliman Yoder.

4 Miroslav Volf, *After Our Likeness: The Church as the Image of the Trinity* (Grand Rapids: Eerdmans, 1998), 145-146, 148-149, 156, 170-171.

5 "Have no part in this folly *(dementia)*." Musurillo, *Acts*, 89.

6 Rodney Clapp, *A Peculiar People: The Church as Culture in a Post-Christian Society* (Downers Grove, IL: InterVarsity Press, 1996), 96-98.

7 Stanley Hauerwas, *The Peaceable Kingdom: A Primer in Christian Ethics* (London: SCM Press, 1984), 100.

8 Craig Dykstra, *Vision and Character: A Christian Education Alternative to Kohlberg* (New York: Paulist Press, 1981), 52.

9 Alasdair MacIntyre, *After Virtue: A Study in Moral Theory*, second edition (Notre Dame: University of Notre Dame Press, 1984), 208, 216.

10 Robert Bellah, Richard Madsen, William M. Sullivan, Ann Swidler, and Steven M. Tipton, eds., *Habits of the Heart: Individualism and Commitment in American Life*, First California paperback edition (Berkeley: University of California Press, 1996), 81.

11 Stanley Hauerwas, *A Community of Character: Toward a Constructive Christian Social Ethic* (Notre Dame: University of Notre Dame Press, 1981), 125-127, 134, 136, 144-147, 151; Harry Huebner, "A Community of Virtues," in *Church As Parable: Whatever Happened to Ethics?*, ed. Harry Huebner and David Schroeder (Winnipeg, MB: CMBC Publications, 1993), 177.

12 Dykstra, *Vision*, 46.

13 Walter Wink, *Engaging the Powers: Discernment and Resistance in a World of Domination* (Minneapolis: Fortress Press, 1992), 13; Walter

Brueggemann, *Theology of the Old Testament: Testimony, Dispute, Advocacy* (Minneapolis: Fortress Press, 1997), 718.

14 Wink, *Engaging*, 304.

15 Miroslav Volf, "The Clumsy Embrace," *Christianity Today*, October 26, 1998, 69.

16 Romans 16:16; 1 Thessalonians 5:26; 2 Peter 5:14; Justin Martyr, 1 *Apol* 65.2; Tertullian, *On Prayer* 18; *Apostolic Tradition* 18. For comment, see Eleanor Kreider, "Let the Faithful Greet Each Other: The Kiss of Peace," *Conrad Grebel Review*, 5.1 (1987), 29-49.

17 *Didascalia Apostolorum*, 2.54, 2.56; see Alan Kreider, "Peacemaking in the Syrian Church Orders," *Studia Liturgica*, 34.2 (2004), 177-190.

18 Eleanor Kreider, *Communion Shapes Character* (Scottdale, PA: Herald Press, 1997).

19 Clapp, *Peculiar People*, 110-111.

20 Steve Finamore, "Worship, Social Action and the Kingdom of Heaven," *Theology Themes* 4.2. (1997), 8-12.

Chapter 7

1 Stanley Hauerwas, *Christian Existence Today: Essays on Church, World, and Living In Between* (Durham, NC: Labyrinth Press, 1988), 95.

2 Stanley Hauerwas, *Vision and Virtue: Essays in Christian Ethical Reflection* (Notre Dame: Fides Publishers, 1974), 35.

3 Ibid., 20, 79.

4 Craig Dykstra, *Vision and Character: A Christian Education Alternative to Kohlberg* (New York: Paulist Press, 1981), 58.

5 Stanley Hauerwas, *Character and the Christian Life: A Study in Theological Ethics* (Notre Dame: Notre Dame University Press, 1994), 223-224.

6 James Wm. McClendon, Jr., *Systematic Theology: Ethics*, 1 (Nashville: Abingdon Press, 1986), 90.

7 Miroslav Volf, *Exclusion and Embrace: A Theological Exploration of Identity, Otherness, and Reconciliation* (Nashville: Abingdon Press, 1996), 213, 256.

8 1 Corinthians 12:3; 14:29; 1 Thessalonians 5:21; 2 Peter 1:20; 1 John 4:1.

9 John Bender, "Reconciliation Begins in Canada," *Mennonite Central Committee Peace Section Newsletter*, 16 (Jan.-Feb. 1986), 1-3.

10 Esther K. Augsburger, "Guns into Plowshares—a Sculpture for Peace" (typescript). The other sculptor is Michael Augsburger.

11 Walter Wink, *When the Powers Fall: Reconciliation in the Healing of Nations*. (Minneapolis: Fortress Press, 1998), 62-63.

12 Max L. Stackhouse, *Public Theology and Political Economy: Christian Stewardship in Modern Society* (Grand Rapids: Eerdmans, 1987), 113-137.

13 Thomas Gordon, *Discipline That Works: Promoting Self-Discipline in Children* (New York: Plume, 1991).

14 John Perkins, *With Justice for All* (Ventura, CA: Regal Books, 1982). For insightful comment see Mark R. Gornick, *To Live in Peace: Biblical Faith and the Changing Inner City* (Grand Rapids: Eerdmans, 2002), 167, ff.

15 The American Catholic bishops realized this in *The Challenge of Peace,* their 1983 pastoral letter on war and peace, section 318: "Those who in conscience decide that they should no longer be associated with defense activities should find support in the Catholic community" (Philip J. Murnion, ed., *Catholics and Nuclear War* (Maryknoll, NY: Orbis Books, 1983), 332.

16 Christmas letter from David Cockburn, December 18, 1997.

Chapter 8

1 Alan Kreider, "Christ, Culture, and Truth-Telling," *Conrad Grebel Review,* 15.3 (1997), 207-208.

2 Shet Sonwani, Report to the Peace Council, Mennonite World Conference, Bihar Mennonite Mandali, October 24, 2002.

3 Ronald J. Sider, *Completely Pro-Life: Building a Consistent Stance* (Downers Grove, IL: InterVarsity Press, 1987); Joseph Cardinal Bernardin, *Consistent Ethic of Life* (Kansas City: Sheed & Ward, 1988); Jim Wallis, *God's Politics: A New Vision for Faith and Politics in America* (San Francisco: Harper San Francisco), chapter 18, "A Consistent Ethics of Life"; Darrin W. Belousek, "Toward a Consistent Ethic of Life in Peace Church Perspective," *Mennonite Quarterly Review,* forthcoming.

4 Intercourse, PA: Good Books, 2003.

5 Exceptionally influential writing by Mennonites includes, John Howard Yoder, *The Politics of Jesus: Vicit Agnus Noster* (Grand Rapids: Eerdmans, 1972; rev. ed., 1994); Ron Sider, *Rich Christians in an Age of Hunger* (Downers Grove, IL: InterVarsity Press, 1977, with many subsequent editions); and by the inspirer of the World Council of Churches' Decade to Overcome Violence, Fernando Enns, *Friedenskirche in der Ökumene: Mennonitische Wurzeln einer Ethik der Gewaltfreiheit* (Peace Church within the Ecumenical Movement: The Mennonite Roots of an Ethic of Nonviolence) (Göttingen: Vandenhoeck & Ruprecht, 2003).

6 Alan Kreider and Stuart Murray, eds., *Coming Home: Stories of Anabaptists in Britain and Ireland* (Kitchener, ON: Pandora Press, 2000).

7 Juan Francisco Martinez, "Latin American Anabaptist-Mennonites: A Profile," *Mennonite Quarterly Review,* 74.3 (2000), 474n. Martinez adds: "Often people like the 'Pentecostal Anabaptists' . . . have a clearer 'Anabaptist perspective' than many Mennonites."

8 Roland H. Bainton, *Christian Attitudes toward War and Peace: A Historical Survey and Critical Re-Evaluation.* (Nashville: Abingdon, 1960).

9 For the origin of the term "Blank Check," see John H. Yoder, *Christian Attitudes Toward War, Peace and Revolution: A Companion to Bainton* (Elkhart, IN: Co-Op Bookstore, 1983), 82.

10 Alan Kreider, "Military Service in the Church Orders." *Journal of Religious Ethics*, 31.3 (2003), 415-442.

11 Bainton, *Christian Attitudes*, chapter 6.

12 These criteria, as in Appendix II, are those of the American Catholic Bishops in their 1983 pastoral letter, *The Challenge of Peace* (in Murnion, *Catholics and Nuclear War*). But they are very similar to those of Protestant Christians, such as the Evangelical philosopher Arthur F. Holmes of Wheaton College: "A Just War: Defining Some Key Issues," in Oliver Barclay, ed., *Pacifism and War: When Christians Disagree* (Leicester, UK: Inter-Varsity Press, 1984), 27-30. The Just War is a Christendom tradition that unites most Catholics and Protestants.

13 From the era of the Vietnam War, see James E. Finn, ed., *Conflict of Loyalties: The Case for Selective Conscientious Objection* (Nashville: Abingdon Press, 1971); from the era of the Iraq War, see "Selective Conscientious Objection: History, Theology and Practice," *The Sign of Peace*, 4.2 (Spring, 2005), 16-21. See also from members of the Latin American Theological Fraternity, C. René Padilla and Lindy Scott, "The War in Iraq; How Just Was This War?" in their *Terrorism and the War in Iraq: A Christian Word from Latin America* (Buenos Aires, Argentina: Kairos Ediciones, 2004) chapter 2.

14 Evangelical Christians who are nuclear pacifists include the beloved Evangelical theologian/statesman John Stott—"[Because strategic nuclear weapons are] indiscriminate in their effects . . . they are ethically indefensible, and . . . every Christian, whatever he may think of the possibility of a 'just' use of conventional weapons, must be a nuclear pacifist" (*Christianity Today*, February 8, 1980). (For a more nuanced statement of his position, see Stott, *Issues Facing Christians Today [London: Collins, 1990]*, chapter 5, "The Nuclear Threat.") They also include philosopher Arthur F. Holmes of Wheaton College—"Complete nuclear abstinence, usually called 'nuclear pacifism,' is [in view of the danger of the likely use of nuclear weapons against cities filled with civilians] the only prudent course to follow in terms of a just war" ("A Just War," 31).

15 John Howard Yoder, *When War Is Unjust: Being Honest in Just-War Thinking* (Maryknoll, NY: Orbis Books, 1996).

16 Glen H. Stassen, *Just Peacemaking: Transforming Initiatives for Justice and Peace* (Cleveland: Pilgrim Press, 1998), passim, and especially page 29.

17 Lesslie Newbigin, *The Other Side of 1984: Questions for the Churches* (Geneva: World Council of Churches, 1983), 1.

Chapter 9

1 Report to Mennonite World Conference Peace Council, from CIEMN (Nicaragua), 2003.

2 Warwick District Council Working Document, "Criteria for Membership in Tidewater Area Mennonite Churches," January 21, 1991; "Response to Issues Raised by Norfolk and Warwick Districts," Faith and Life Commission, Virginia Mennonite Conference, April 1, 1995; Steve Fannin, "Must Churches Exclude Warriors?" *Mennonite Weekly Review*, March 30, 1995, 1-2; "Understandings for Staff Persons and Oversight Committee/Board, Alternatives to Military Career Program in Tidewater, Virginia," March 19, 2000. We are grateful to Gordon D. Zook for this information.

3 *Apostolic Tradition* [attributed to Hippolytus], 16.9: "A soldier who has authority, let him not kill a man. If he is ordered, let him not go to the task, nor let him swear. But if he is not willing, let him be cast out [rejected as a baptismal candidate]." The document continued by forbidding catechumens or believers to join the forces: "A catechumen or faithful person, if he wishes to become a soldier, let him be cast out because he has despised God." Paul F. Bradshaw, Maxwell E. Johnson, L. Edward Phillips, eds., *Apostolic Tradition: A Commentary* (Minneapolis: Fortress Press, 2002), 90.

4 Lois Y. Barrett, ed., *Treasure in Clay Jars: Patterns in Missional Faithfulness* (Grand Rapids: Eerdmans, 2004), 49, 82.

5 Ron Sider, Philip N. Olson and Heidi Rolland Unruh, *Churches That Make a Difference* (Grand Rapids: Baker Books, 2002); Mark R. Gornik, *To Live in Peace: Biblical Faith and the Changing Inner City* (Grand Rapids: Eerdmans, 2002).

6 Robert Warren, *Being Human, Being Church* (London: Marshall Pickering, 1995), 154.

7 Darrell R. Guder, *Missional Church: A Vision for the Sending of the Church in North America* (Grand Rapids: Eerdmans, 1998), 108.

8 Barrett, *Treasure*, 85.

9 John Howard Yoder, *Body Politics: Five Practices of the Christian Community Before the Watching World* (Scottdale, PA: Herald Press), 2001.

10 *Reconciliation as the Mission of God: Faithful Christian Witness in a World of Destructive Conflicts and Divisions*, Issue Group on Reconciliation (47 Christian leaders [including Paulus S. Widjaja] from 21 countries), one of 31 issue groups under the umbrella of the Lausanne Committee on World Evangelization, Pattya, Thailand, September-October 2004, endorsed January 2005, section III; available from www.reconcilationnetwork.com.

11 For an example of sound missionary reflection and practice in an Islamic culture, see Gordon Nickel, *Peaceable Witness Among Muslims* (Scottdale, PA: Herald Press, 1999).

12 Robert L. Ramseyer, "Mennonite Missions and the Christian Peace Witness." In idem, ed., *Mission and the Peace Witness* (Scottdale, PA: Herald Press, 1979), 114-135.

13 Miroslav Volf, "A Vision of Embrace: Theological Perspectives on Cultural Identity and Conflict," *Ecumenical Review* 47.2 (1995), 195; idem, "The Social Meaning of Reconciliation," *Interpretation* 54.2 (2000), 158.

14 David W. Shenk, *Justice, Reconciliation and Peace in Africa* (Nairobi: Uzima, 1997), 134-136.

15 *Reconciliation as the Mission of God* (see note 10 above), section IV, conclusion and recommendation 1.

16 John Stott gives this in oral presentations as a kind of "dictum" when presenting a rationale for the Langham Ministries of which he is founder. Email from Chris Wright to Paulus Widjaja, May 31, 2005.

17 *Reconciliation as the Mission of God* (see note 10 above), section II (italics in the original). This statement was accompanied by the following footnote: "In South Africa, for example, the 'homogeneous unit principle' was popular among Christians who supported apartheid. In India, leading advocates of church growth often tacitly accepted caste divisions; in the U.S. the same has happened regarding racial and ethnic divisions."

18 Ibid., section II.

19 Arthur Paul Boers, "Pastors, Prophets, and Patriotism: Leading Pastorally during These Times," in Wes Avram, ed., *Anxious About Empire: Theological Essays on the New Global Realities* (Grand Rapids: Brazos, 2004), 167.

20 Judy Zimmerman Herr, "Perspective: Professional Peacemakers," *Courier*, 19.3 (2004), 16.

21 Dallas Willard, *The Divine Conspiracy: Rediscovering Our Hidden Life in God* (San Francisco: Harper San Francisco, 1998), 244.

Scripture Index

About the Authors

Alan Kreider has spent his life in Christian mission and peace-making. He was born in Indiana, grew up in Japan, and has spent most of his adult life in England, where for 26 years he was a missionary with Mennonite Board of Missions. He has taught widely in Europe and North America and in recent years has frequently taught in Asia and Australia. He is especially happy when teaching together with his wife, Eleanor.

Alan was educated at Goshen (IN) College and Harvard University, where he completed a Ph.D. in English Reformation history (*English Chantries: The Road to Dissolution* [Harvard University Press, 1979]). He is author of *Journey Toward Holiness* (Herald Press, 1987), an award-winning book on Christian discipleship, and has written and edited more than 10 books and numerous articles in areas of mission, peacemaking, and church history. In the past 20 years he has retooled himself as a scholar of the early church, about which he loves to teach because of its relevance to Christians today. A representative product of his early church scholarship is *The Change of Conversion and the Origin of Christendom* (Trinity Press International, 1999).

Alan is Associate Professor of Church History and Mission at Associated Mennonite Biblical Seminary, Elkhart, IN, Mission Educator for the Mennonite Mission Network, and an ordained minister in the Mennonite Church. Together with Eleanor, he was for many years co-director of the London Mennonite Centre in England. In England he was active in the peace movement and taught at London Bible College and Northern Baptist College. Between 1995 and 2000 he was founding director of the Centre for the Study of Christianity and Culture, Regent's Park College, Oxford University.

Eleanor Kreider grew up as a child of Mennonite missionaries in India and cherishes a love and commitment to global Christian mission. She was trained as a musician at Goshen (IN) College and the University of Michigan, Ann Arbor. After teaching for several years at Goshen College she pursued her interest in the theology and practice of worship with studies at the University of Notre Dame and King's College, London. She has taught extensively at seminaries and church conferences in England and North America, as well as in New Zealand, Australia, Taiwan, Hong Kong, and Japan. She is Adjunct Faculty in Worship and Mission at Associated Mennonite Biblical Seminary, and Mission Educator for Mennonite Mission Network.

Eleanor is author of *Enter His Gates: Fitting Worship Together* (Herald Press, 1990) and *Communion Shapes Character* (Herald Press, 1995). Her characteristic emphases are to deepen corporate prayer, to develop a rich use of Scripture in worship, and to encourage more frequent and life-giving communion services. A current project is her work with an editorial team on *Take Our Moments and Our Days: An Anabaptist Prayerbook* (in preparation for publication).

For 26 years Eleanor and her husband, Alan Kreider, served as Mennonite missionaries in England, where they were involved in establishing a Mennonite church and the nationwide Anabaptist Network. During their years as directors, the London Mennonite Centre emerged as a place of teaching and resourcing in Christian discipleship in the Anabaptist tradition. The Kreiders received a wide hearing in the United Kingdom as peace advocates and teachers of peacemaking theology and practice.

Eleanor and Alan are members of Prairie Street Mennonite Church, Elkhart, IN. They are parents of Andrew Kreider, who is pastor of their church, who with his wife Katie have three children, Joe, Dan, and Rosie.

Paulus Widjaja holds major positions in peace-related efforts in his native Indonesia. He is a lecturer on the faculty of theology at Duta Wacana Christian University in Jogjakarta, Central Java, teaching ethics and peacebuilding. Paulus completed an M.A. in Peace Studies from Associated Mennonite Biblical Seminary, Elkhart, IN. His Ph.D. is in theological ethics from Fuller Theological Seminary, School of Theology, Pasadena, CA.

He is Director of the Center for the Study and Promotion of Peace, also at Duta Wacana Christian University (www.ukdw.ac.id/pspp/). In that capacity he oversees and participates in trainings in mediation and conflict transformation, offered to those who live in Indonesia, as well as throughout Asia/Pacific. The Center's services are used by a broad public made up of many religious groups (including Christians, Muslims, and Hindus), by many ethnic communities, and by a variety of professionals, among them government officials and leaders of NGOs. The Center also offers trainings geared to women and trainings for children.

Following the 2004 tsunami, Paulus became chairman of a collaborative effort in Indonesia, which provides trauma healing and conflict transformation training. This civil society organization is made up of several religious communities and has so far focused on Aceh and Nias, both in Indonesia.

Since 1993, Paulus has been the Peace Council Secretary for Mennonite World Conference, a worldwide community of Anabaptist-related churches.

He is also an advisor for the Muria Academy, a training center for potential pastors, operated by the GKMI Synod of the Indonesia Mennonite church.

Paulus' wife, Janti, is the pastor of a Mennonite congregation in Jogjakarta. Paulus and Janti are the parents of a daughter, Mitha, and a son, Dhika.